The Iron Wall

We and the Arabs

1923

Vladimir Ze'ev Jabotinsky

It is an excellent rule to begin an article with the most important point, but this time, I find it necessary to start with an introduction and, in addition, with a personal presentation.

I have the reputation of being an enemy of the Arabs, who wants them to be expelled from Palestine, etc. That is not true.

Emotionally, my attitude towards Arabs is the same as towards all other nations: polite indifference.

Politically, my attitude is determined by two principles.

In the first place, I consider it absolutely impossible to expel the Arabs from Palestine. There will always be two nations in Palestine, which is good enough for me, as long as the Jews become the majority. And, secondly, I belong to the group that once worked out the Helsingfors Program, the program of national rights for all nationalities living in the same state.

In drawing up that program, we had in mind not only the Jews, but all nations everywhere, and its basis is equal rights.

I am willing to take an oath that commits ourselves and our descendants that we will never do anything contrary to the principle of equal rights and that we will never attempt to expel anyone.

This seems to me to be a rather peaceful creed.

But it is quite another question whether it is always possible to achieve a peaceful goal by peaceful means. For the answer to this question does not depend on our attitude toward the Arabs, but entirely on the attitude of the Arabs toward us and toward Zionism.

Now, after this introduction, we can move on to the subject.

A voluntary agreement is not possible

There can be no voluntary agreement between us and the Palestinian Arabs. Not now and not in the future. I say this with such conviction, not because I want to hurt moderate Zionists. I don't think they will be hurt. Except for those blind from birth, they realized long ago that it is absolutely impossible to obtain the voluntary consent of the Palestinian Arabs to convert "Palestine" from an Arab country to a Jewish majority country.

My readers have a general idea of the history of colonization in other countries. I suggest that they consider all the precedents they know and see if there is an isolated case of any colonization taking place with the consent of the native population. There is no such precedent.

Native populations, civilized or uncivilized, have always stubbornly resisted the settlers, no matter whether they were civilized or savages.

And it did not matter whether the settlers behaved decently or not.

The companions of Cortez and Pizzaro, or (as some will remind us) our own ancestors under Joshua Ben Nun, behaved like bandits; but the Pilgrim Fathers, the first true pioneers of North America, were people of the highest morality, who meant no harm to anyone, least of all the Red Indians, and honestly believed that there was enough room on the prairies for both the Paleface and the Redskin. However, the native population fought just as fiercely against the good settlers as against the bad ones.

Every native population, civilized or not, regards its lands as its national home, of which it is the sole owner, and wants to retain that dominion always; it will refuse to admit not only new masters, but also new partners or collaborators.

The Arabs are not fools

This is equally true for the Arabs.

Our pacifists are trying to persuade us that the Arabs are fools, whom we can fool by masking our true objectives, or that they are corrupt and can be bribed to give up their claim to priority in Palestine in exchange for cultural policy and economic advantages.

I repudiate this conception of the Palestinian Arabs.

Culturally they are five hundred years behind us, they do not have our stamina or our determination; but they are as good psychologists like us, and their minds have been sharpened like ours by centuries of finely woven logomachy.

We can tell them what we like about the innocence of our aims, diluting and sweetening them with honeyed words to make them agreeable, but they know what we want, just as we know what they do not want.

They feel at least the same instinctive and jealous love for Palestine as the old Aztecs felt for ancient Mexico, and the Sioux for their rolling prairies.

To imagine, as do our friends of the Arabs, that they would willingly consent to the realization of Zionism, in exchange for the moral and material comforts that the Jewish settler brings with him, is a childish notion, which at bottom has a kind of contempt for the Arab People; it means that they despise the Arab race, which they consider a corrupt mob that can be bought and sold, and are ready to give up their homeland for a good railway system.

All natives resist settlers

There is no justification for such a belief. It may be that some Arabs take bribes. But this does not mean that the Arab people of Palestine as a whole sell out that fervent patriotism which they guard so zealously and which even the Papuans will never sell out.

Every native population in the world resists the settlers as long as it has the slightest hope of being able to free itself from the danger of being colonized.

That is what the Arabs are doing in Palestine, and what they will continue to do as long as there remains a single spark of hope that they will be able to prevent the transformation of "Palestine" into the "Land of Israel".

Arab understanding

Some of us have been led to believe that the whole problem is due to a misunderstanding: the Arabs have not understood us, and that is the only reason why they resist us; if we can only make it clear to them how moderate our intentions really are, they will immediately extend their hand to us in friendship.

This belief is completely unfounded and has been destroyed time and again. I will recall only one example of many. Some years ago, when the late Mr. Sokolow was on one of his periodic visits to Palestine, he addressed a meeting on this very question of "misunderstanding." He lucidly and convincingly demonstrated that the Arabs are terribly mistaken if they think that we have any desire to deprive them of their possessions or to expel them from the country, or that we want to oppress them. We do not even ask that a Jewish government uphold the mandate of the League of Nations.

One of the Arab newspapers, "The Carmel," responded at that time, in an editorial article, the meaning of which was as follows: The Zionists are making a fuss over nothing. There is no misunderstanding. All that Sokolow says about Zionist intentions is true, but the Arabs know it without him. Of course, the Zionists cannot now think of expelling the Arabs from the country or oppressing them, they do not contemplate a Jewish government. Obviously, they are now concerned with only one thing: that the Arabs do not hinder their immigration. The Zionists assure us that even immigration will be regulated strictly according to the economic needs of Palestine. The Arabs have never doubted that: it is a truism, for otherwise there can be no immigration.

No "misunderstandings"

This Arab editor was actually willing to agree that Palestine has a very large potential absorption capacity, which means that there is room for a large number of Jews in the country without displacing a single Arab. There is only one thing that the Zionists want, and that is the one thing that the Arabs don't want, because that is the way the Jews would gradually become the majority, and then a government Jewish would automatically follow, and the future of the Arab minority would depend on the goodwill of the Jews; and minority status is not a good thing, as the Jews themselves never tire of pointing out. So there is no "misunderstanding."

The Zionists want only one thing, Jewish immigration; and this Jewish immigration is what the Arabs do not want.

This statement of the Arab publisher's position is so logical, so obvious, so indisputable, that everyone should know it by heart and it should be the basis of all our future discussions on the Arab question.

It matters not at all what phraseology we employ to explain our colonizing aims, Herzl or Sir Herbert Samuel. Colonization has its own explanation, the only possible explanation, unalterable and as clear as daylight to every ordinary Jew and every ordinary Arab.

Colonization can have only one goal and the Palestinian Arabs cannot accept it. It lies in the very nature of things and, in this particular respect, nature cannot change.

The Iron Wall

We cannot offer any adequate compensation to the Palestinian Arabs in exchange for Palestine. And, therefore, there is no likelihood that any voluntary agreement will be reached. So all those who consider such an agreement as a sine qua non for Zionism can also say "no" and withdraw from Zionism.

Zionist colonization can continue and develop only under the protection of a power that is independent of the native population, behind an iron wall, which the native population cannot break through.

That is our Arab policy; not what we should be, but what it really is, whether we admit it or not. What need, otherwise, of the Balfour Declaration? Or of the

Mandate? Its value to us is that the outside Power has undertaken to create in the country such conditions of administration and security that, should the native population wish to hinder our work, will find it impossible.

And all of us, without exception, demand day by day that this external power carry out this task with vigor and determination.

In this matter there is no difference between our "militarists" and our "vegetarians". Except that the former prefer the iron wall to be manned by Jewish soldiers, and the others are content that it should be British.

We all demand that there be an iron wall. Yet we keep messing up our own case, talking about "agreement," which means to tell the Government that the important thing is not the iron wall, but the discussions. This guy's empty rhetoric is dangerous. And that is why it is not only a pleasure but a duty to discredit him and show that he is fantastic and dishonest.

Moral and just Zionism

Two brief remarks:

First, if anyone objects that this view is immoral, I reply that it is not true: either Zionism is moral and just, or it is immoral and unfair. But that is a question we should have resolved before we became Zionists. Actually, we have resolved that question, and in the affirmative.

We hold that Zionism is moral and just. And since it is moral and just, justice must be done, regardless of whether Joseph, Simon, Ivan or Achmet agree or disagree.

There is no other morality.

Eventual agreement

Secondly, this does not mean that there can be no agreement with the Palestinian Arabs. What is impossible is a voluntary agreement. As long as the Arabs feel that there is the slightest hope of getting rid of us, they will refuse to give up this hope in exchange for kind words or bread and butter, because they are not a rabble, but a living people. And when a living people give in on matters of such vital importance it is only when there is no longer any hope of getting rid of us, because they cannot breach the iron wall. Until then they will not abandon their extremist leaders, whose slogan is "Never!" And the leadership will pass to the moderate groups, who will approach us with a proposal for both of us to agree on mutual concessions. Then we can expect them to honestly discuss practical issues, such as a guarantee against Arab displacement, equal rights for Arab citizens, or Arab national integrity.

And when that happens, I am convinced that we Jews will be ready to give them satisfactory guarantees, so that both peoples can live together in peace, as good neighbors.

But the only way to obtain such an agreement is the iron wall, i.e., a strong power in Palestine that is not susceptible to any Arab pressure. In other words, the only way to reach an agreement in the future is to abandon any idea of seeking an agreement in the present.

The Jewish State

by

Theodor Herzl

Preface

The idea which I have developed in this pamphlet is a very old one: it is the restoration of the Jewish State.

The world resounds with outcries against the Jews, and these outcries have awakened the slumbering idea.

I wish it to be clearly understood from the outset that no portion of my argument is based on a new discovery. I have discovered neither the historic condition of the Jews nor the means to improve it. In fact, every man will see for himself that the materials of the structure I am designing are not only in existence, but actually already in hand. If, therefore, this attempt to solve the Jewish Question is to be designated by a single word, let it be said to be the result of an inescapable conclusion rather than that of a flighty imagination.

I must, in the first place, guard my scheme from being treated as Utopian by superficial critics who might commit this error of judgment if I did not warn them. I should obviously have done nothing to be ashamed of if I had described a Utopia on philanthropic lines; and I should also, in all probability, have obtained literary success more easily if I had set forth my plan in the irresponsible guise of a romantic tale. But this Utopia is far less attractive than any one of those portrayed by Sir Thomas More and his numerous forerunners and successors. And I believe that the situation of the Jews in many countries is grave enough to make such preliminary trifling superfluous.

An interesting book, "Freiland," by Dr. Theodor Hertzka, which appeared a few years ago, may serve to mark the distinction I draw between my conception and a Utopia. His is the ingenious invention of a modern mind thoroughly schooled in the principles of political economy; it is as remote from actuality as the Equatorial Mountain on which his dream State lies. "Freiland" is a complicated piece of mechanism with numerous cogged wheels fitting into each other; but there is nothing to prove that they can be set in motion. Even supposing "Freiland societies" were to come into existence, I should look on the whole thing as a joke.

The present scheme, on the other hand, includes the employment of an existent propelling force. In consideration of my own inadequacy, I shall content myself with indicating the cogs and wheels of the machine to be constructed, and I shall rely on more skilled technicians than myself to put them together.

Everything depends on our propelling force. And what is that force? The misery of the Jews.

Who would venture to deny its existence? We shall discuss it fully in the chapter on the causes of Anti-Semitism.

Everybody is familiar with the phenomenon of steam-power, generated by boiling water, which lifts the kettle-lid. Such tea-kettle phenomena are the attempts of Zionist and kindred associations to check Anti-Semitism.

I believe that this power, if rightly employed, is powerful enough to propel a large engine and to move passengers and goods: the engine having whatever form men may choose to give it.

I am absolutely convinced that I am right, though I doubt whether I shall live to see myself proved to be so. Those who are the first to inaugurate this movement will scarcely live to see its glorious close. But the inauguration of it is enough to give them a feeling of pride and the joy of spiritual freedom.

I shall not be lavish in artistically elaborated descriptions of my project, for fear of incurring the suspicion of painting a Utopia. I anticipate, in any case, that thoughtless scoffers will caricature my sketch and thus try to weaken its effect. A Jew, intelligent in other respects, to whom I explained my plan, was of the opinion that "a Utopia was a project whose future details were represented as already extant." This is a fallacy. Every Chancellor of the Exchequer calculates in his Budget estimates with assumed figures, and not only with such as are based on the average returns of past years, or on previous revenues in other States, but sometimes with figures for which there is no precedent whatever; as for example, in instituting a new tax. Everybody who studies a Budget knows that this is the case. But even if it were known that the estimates would not be rigidly adhered to, would such a financial draft be considered Utopian?

But I am expecting more of my readers. I ask the cultivated men whom I am addressing to set many preconceived ideas entirely aside. I shall even go so far as to ask those Jews who have most earnestly tried to solve the Jewish Question to look upon their previous attempts as mistaken and futile.

I must guard against a danger in setting forth my idea. If I describe future circumstances with too much caution I shall appear to doubt their possibility. If, on the other hand, I announce their realization with too much assurance I shall appear to be describing a chimera.

I shall therefore clearly and emphatically state that I believe in the practical outcome of my scheme, though without professing to have discovered the shape it may ultimately take. The Jewish State is essential to the world; it will therefore be created.

The plan would, of course, seem absurd if a single individual attempted to do it; but if worked by a number of Jews in co-operation it would appear perfectly rational, and its accomplishment would present no difficulties worth mentioning. The idea depends only on the number of its supporters. Perhaps our ambitious young men, to whom every road of progress is now closed, seeing in this Jewish State a bright prospect of freedom, happiness and honors opening to them, will ensure the propagation of the idea.

I feel that with the publication of this pamphlet my task is done. I shall not again take up the pen, unless the attacks of noteworthy antagonists drive me to do so, or it becomes necessary to meet unforeseen objections and to remove errors.

Am I stating what is not yet the case? Am I before my time? Are the sufferings of the Jews not yet grave enough? We shall see.

It depends on the Jews themselves whether this political pamphlet remains for the present a political romance. If the present generation is too dull to understand it rightly, a future, finer and a better generation will arise to understand it. The Jews who wish for a State shall have it, and they will deserve to have it.

Chapter I. Introduction

It is astonishing how little insight into the science of economics many of the men who move in the midst of active life possess. Hence it is that even Jews faithfully repeat the cry of the Anti-Semites: "We depend for sustenance on the nations who are our hosts, and if we had no hosts to support us we should die of starvation." This is a point that shows how unjust accusations may weaken our self-knowledge. But what are the true grounds for this statement concerning the nations that act as "hosts"? Where it is not based on limited physiocratic views it is founded on the childish error that commodities pass from hand to hand in continuous rotation. We need not wake from long slumber, like Rip van Winkle, to realize that the world is considerably altered by the production of new commodities. The technical progress made during this wonderful era enables even a man of most limited intelligence to note with his short-sighted eyes the appearance of new commodities all around him. The spirit of enterprise has created them.

Labor without enterprise is the stationary labor of ancient days; and typical of it is the work of the husbandman, who stands now just where his progenitors stood a thousand years ago. All our material welfare has been brought about by men of enterprise. I feel almost ashamed of writing down so trite a remark. Even if we were a nation of entrepreneurs—such as absurdly exaggerated accounts make us out to be—we should not require another nation to live on. We do not depend on the circulation of old commodities, because we produce new ones.

The world possesses slaves of extraordinary capacity for work, whose appearance has been fatal to the production of handmade goods: these slaves are the machines. It is true that workmen are required to set machinery in motion; but for this we have men in plenty, in super-abundance. Only those who are ignorant of the conditions of Jews in many countries of Eastern Europe would venture to assert that Jews are either unfit or unwilling to perform manual labor.

But I do not wish to take up the cudgels for the Jews in this pamphlet. It would be useless. Everything rational and everything sentimental that can possibly be said in their defense has been said already. If one's hearers are incapable of comprehending them, one is a preacher in a desert. And if one's hearers are broad and high-minded enough to have grasped them already, then the sermon is superfluous. I believe in the ascent of man to higher and yet higher grades of civilization; but I consider this ascent to be desperately slow. Were we to wait till average humanity had become as charitably inclined as was Lessing when he wrote "Nathan the Wise," we should wait beyond our day, beyond the days of our children, of our grandchildren, and of our great-grandchildren. But the world's spirit comes to our aid in another way.

This century has given the world a wonderful renaissance by means of its technical achievements; but at the same time its miraculous improvements have not been employed in the service of humanity. Distance has ceased to be an obstacle, yet we complain of insufficient space. Our great steamships carry us swiftly and surely over hitherto unvisited seas. Our railways carry us safely into a mountain-world hitherto tremblingly scaled on foot. Events occurring in countries undiscovered when Europe confined the Jews in

Ghettos are known to us in the course of an hour. Hence the misery of the Jews is an anachronism—not because there was a period of enlightenment one hundred years ago, for that enlightenment reached in reality only the choicest spirits.

I believe that electric light was not invented for the purpose of illuminating the drawing-rooms of a few snobs, but rather for the purpose of throwing light on some of the dark problems of humanity. One of these problems, and not the least of them, is the Jewish question. In solving it we are working not only for ourselves, but also for many other over-burdened and oppressed beings.

The Jewish question still exists. It would be foolish to deny it. It is a remnant of the middle Ages, which civilized nations do not even yet seem able to shake off, try as they will. They certainly showed a generous desire to do so when they emancipated us. The Jewish question exists wherever Jews live in perceptible numbers. Where it does not exist, it is carried by Jews in the course of their migrations. We naturally move to those places where we are not persecuted, and there our presence produces persecution. This is the case in every country, and will remain so, even in those highly civilized—for instance, France—until the Jewish question finds a solution on a political basis. The unfortunate Jews are now carrying the seeds of Anti-Semitism into England; they have already introduced it into America.

I believe that I understand Anti-Semitism, which is really a highly complex movement. I consider it from a Jewish standpoint, yet without fear or hatred. I believe that I can see what elements there are in it of vulgar sport, of common trade jealousy, of inherited prejudice, of religious intolerance, and also of pretended self-defense. I think the Jewish question is no more a social than a religious one, notwithstanding that it sometimes takes these and other forms. It is a national question, which can only be solved by making it a political world-question to be discussed and settled by the civilized nations of the world in council.

We are a people—one people.

We have honestly endeavored everywhere to merge ourselves in the social life of surrounding communities and to preserve the faith of our fathers. We are not permitted to do so. In vain are we loyal patriots, our loyalty in some places running to extremes; in vain do we make the same sacrifices of life and property as our fellow-citizens; in vain do we strive to increase the fame of our native land in science and art, or her wealth by trade and commerce. In countries where we have lived for centuries we are still cried down as strangers, and often by those whose ancestors were not yet domiciled in the land where Jews had already had experience of suffering. The majority may decide which are the strangers; for this, as indeed every point which arises in the relations between nations, is a question of might. I do not here surrender any portion of our prescriptive right, when I make this statement merely in my own name as an individual. In the world as it now is and for an indefinite period will probably remain, might precedes right. It is useless, therefore, for us to be loyal patriots, as were the Huguenots who were forced to emigrate. If we could only be left in peace....

But I think we shall not be left in peace.

Oppression and persecution cannot exterminate us. No nation on earth has survived such struggles and sufferings as we have gone through. Jew-baiting has merely stripped off our weaklings; the strong among us were invariably true to their race when persecution broke out against them. This attitude was most clearly apparent in the period immediately following the emancipation of the Jews. Those Jews who were advanced intellectually and materially entirely lost the feeling of belonging to their race. Wherever our political well-being has lasted for any length of time, we have assimilated with our surroundings. I think this is not discreditable. Hence, the statesman who would wish to see a Jewish strain in his nation would have to provide for the duration of our political well-being; and even a Bismarck could not do that.

For old prejudices against us still lie deep in the hearts of the people. He who would have proofs of this need only listen to the people where they speak with frankness and simplicity: proverb and fairy-tale are both Anti-Semitic. A nation is everywhere a great child, which can certainly be educated; but its education would, even in most favorable circumstances, occupy such a vast amount of time that we could, as already mentioned, remove our own difficulties by other means long before the process was accomplished.

Assimilation, by which I understood not only external conformity in dress, habits, customs, and language, but also identity of feeling and manner—assimilation of Jews could be effected only by intermarriage. But the need for mixed marriages would have to be felt by the majority; their mere recognition by law would certainly not suffice.

The Hungarian Liberals, who have just given legal sanction to mixed marriages, have made a remarkable mistake which one of the earliest cases clearly illustrates; a baptized Jew married a Jewess. At the same time the struggle to obtain the present form of marriage accentuated distinctions between Jews and Christians, thus hindering rather than aiding the fusion of races.

Those who really wished to see the Jews disappear through intermixture with other nations, can only hope to see it come about in one way. The Jews must previously acquire economic power sufficiently great to overcome the old social prejudice against them. The aristocracy may serve as an example of this, for in its ranks occur the proportionately largest numbers of mixed marriages. The Jewish families which regild the old nobility with their money become gradually absorbed. But what form would this phenomenon assume in the middle classes, where (the Jews being a bourgeois people) the Jewish question is mainly concentrated? A previous acquisition of power could be synonymous with that economic supremacy which Jews are already erroneously declared to possess. And if the power they now possess creates rage and indignation among the Anti-Semites, what outbreaks would such an increase of power create? Hence the first step towards absorption will never be taken, because this step would involve the subjection of the majority to a hitherto scorned minority, possessing neither military nor administrative power of its own. I think, therefore, that the absorption of Jews by means of their prosperity is unlikely to occur. In countries which now are Anti-Semitic my view will be approved. In others, where Jews now feel comfortable, it will probably be violently disputed by them. My happier co-religionists will not believe me till Jew-baiting teaches them the truth; for the longer Anti-Semitism lies in abeyance the more fiercely will it break out. The infiltration of immigrating Jews, attracted to a land by apparent security, and the ascent in the social scale of native Jews, combine powerfully to bring about a revolution. Nothing is plainer than this rational conclusion.

Because I have drawn this conclusion with complete indifference to everything but the quest of truth, I shall probably be contradicted and opposed by Jews who are in easy circumstances. Insofar as private interests alone are held by their anxious or timid possessors to be in danger, they can safely be ignored, for the concerns of the poor and oppressed are of greater importance than theirs. But I wish from the outset to prevent any misconception from arising, particularly the mistaken notion that my project, if realized, would in the least degree injure property now held by Jews. I shall therefore explain everything connected with rights of property very fully. Whereas, if my plan never becomes anything more than a piece of literature, things will merely remain as they are. It might more reasonably be objected that I am giving a handle to Anti-Semitism when I say we are a people—one people; that I am hindering the assimilation of Jews where it is about to be consummated, and endangering it where it is an accomplished fact, insofar as it is possible for a solitary writer to hinder or endanger anything.

This objection will be especially brought forward in France. It will probably also be made in other countries, but I shall answer only the French Jews beforehand, because these afford the most striking example of my point.

However much I may worship personality—powerful individual personality in statesmen, inventors, artists, philosophers, or leaders, as well as the collective personality of a historic group of human beings, which we call a nation—however much I may worship personality, I do not regret its disappearance. Whoever can, will, and must perish, let him perish. But the distinctive nationality of Jews neither can, will, nor must be destroyed. It cannot be destroyed, because external enemies consolidate it. It will not be destroyed; this is shown during two thousand years of appalling suffering. It must not be destroyed, and that, as a descendant of numberless Jews who refused to despair, I am trying once more to prove in this pamphlet. Whole branches of Judaism may wither and fall, but the trunk will remain.

Hence, if all or any of the French Jews protest against this scheme on account of their own "assimilation," my answer is simple: The whole thing does not concern them at all. They are Jewish Frenchmen, well and good! This is a private affair for the Jews alone.

The movement towards the organization of the State I am proposing would, of course, harm Jewish Frenchmen no more than it would harm the "assimilated" of other countries. It would, on the contrary, be distinctly to their advantage. For they would no longer be disturbed in their "chromatic function," as Darwin puts it, but would be able to assimilate in peace, because the present Anti-Semitism would have been stopped forever. They would certainly be credited with being assimilated to the very depths of their souls, if they stayed where they were after the new Jewish State, with its superior institutions, had become a reality.

The "assimilated" would profit even more than Christian citizens by the departure of faithful Jews; for they would be rid of the disquieting, incalculable, and unavoidable rivalry of a Jewish proletariat, driven by poverty and political pressure from place to place, from land to land. This floating proletariat would become stationary. Many Christian citizens—whom we call Anti-Semites—can now offer determined resistance to the immigration of foreign Jews. Jewish citizens cannot do this, although it affects them far more directly; for on them they feel first of all the keen competition of individuals carrying on similar branches of industry, who, in addition, either introduce Anti-Semitism where it does not exist, or intensify it where it does. The "assimilated" give expression to this secret grievance in "philanthropic" undertakings. They organize emigration societies for wandering Jews. There is a reverse to the picture which would be comic, if it did not deal with human beings. For some of these charitable institutions are created not for, but against, persecuted Jews; they are created to dispatch these poor creatures just as fast and far as possible. And thus, many an apparent friend of the Jews turns out, on careful inspection, to be nothing more than an Anti-Semite of Jewish origin, disguised as a philanthropist.

But the attempts at colonization made even by really benevolent men, interesting attempts though they were, have so far been unsuccessful. I do not think that this or that man took up the matter merely as an amusement, that they engaged in the emigration of poor Jews as one indulges in the racing of horses. The matter was too grave and tragic for such treatment. These attempts were interesting, in that they represented on a small scale the practical fore-runners of the idea of a Jewish State. They were even useful, for out of their mistakes may be gathered experience for carrying the idea out successfully on a larger scale. They have, of course, done harm also. The transportation of Anti-Semitism to new districts, which is the inevitable consequence of such artificial infiltration, seems to me to be the least of these evils. Far worse is the circumstance that unsatisfactory results tend to cast doubts on intelligent men. What is impractical or impossible to simple argument will remove this doubt from the minds of intelligent men. What is unpractical or impossible to accomplish on a small scale, need not necessarily be so on a larger one. A small enterprise may result in loss under the same conditions which would make a large one pay. A rivulet cannot even be navigated by boats, the river into which it flows carries stately iron vessels.

No human being is wealthy or powerful enough to transplant a nation from one habitation to another. An idea alone can achieve that and this idea of a State may have the requisite power to do so. The Jews have dreamt this kingly dream all through the long nights of their history. "Next year in Jerusalem" is our old phrase. It is now a question of showing that the dream can be converted into a living reality.

For this, many old, outgrown, confused and limited notions must first be entirely erased from the minds of men. Dull brains might, for instance, imagine that this exodus would be from civilized regions into the desert. That is not the case. It will be carried out in the midst of civilization. We shall not revert to a lower stage, we shall rise to a higher one. We shall not dwell in mud huts; we shall build new more beautiful and more modern houses, and possess them in safety. We shall not lose our acquired possessions; we shall realize them. We shall surrender our well earned rights only for better ones. We shall not sacrifice our beloved customs; we shall find them again. We shall not leave our old home before the new one is prepared for us. Those only will depart who are sure thereby to improve their position; those who are now desperate will go first, after them the poor; next the prosperous, and, last of all, the wealthy. Those who go in advance will raise themselves to a higher grade, equal to those whose representatives will shortly follow. Thus the exodus will be at the same time an ascent of the class.

The departure of the Jews will involve no economic disturbances, no crises, no persecutions; in fact, the countries they abandon will revive to a new period of prosperity. There will be an inner migration of Christian citizens into the positions evacuated by Jews. The outgoing current will be gradual, without any disturbance, and its initial movement will put an end to Anti-Semitism. The Jews will leave as honored friends, and if some of them return, they will receive the same favorable welcome and treatment at the hands of civilized nations as is accorded to all foreign visitors. Their exodus will have no resemblance to a flight, for it will be a well-regulated movement under control of public opinion. The movement will not only be inaugurated with absolute conformity to law, but it cannot even be carried out without the friendly cooperation of interested Governments, who would derive considerable benefits from it.

Security for the integrity of the idea and the vigor of its execution will be found in the creation of a body corporate, or corporation. This corporation will be called "The Society of Jews." In addition to it there will be a Jewish company, an economically productive body.

An individual who attempted even to undertake this huge task alone would be either an impostor or a madman. The personal character of the members of the corporation will guarantee its integrity, and the adequate capital of the Company will prove its stability.

These prefatory remarks are merely intended as a hasty reply to the mass of objections which the very words "Jewish State" are certain to arouse. Henceforth we shall proceed more slowly to meet further objections and to explain in detail what has been as yet only indicated; and we shall try in the interests of this pamphlet to avoid making it a dull exposition. Short aphoristic chapters will therefore best answer the purpose.

If I wish to substitute a new building for an old one, I must demolish before I construct. I shall therefore keep to this natural sequence. In the first and general part I shall explain my ideas, remove all prejudices, determine essential political and economic conditions, and develop the plan.

In the special part, which is divided into three principal sections, I shall describe its execution. These three sections are: The Jewish Company, Local Groups, and the Society of Jews. The Society is to be created first, the Company last; but in this exposition the reverse order is preferable, because it is the financial soundness of the enterprise which will chiefly be called into question, and doubts on this score must be removed first.

In the conclusion, I shall try to meet every further objection that could possibly be made. My Jewish readers will, I hope, follow me patiently to the end. Some will naturally make their objections in an order of succession other than that chosen for their refutation. But whoever finds his doubts dispelled should give allegiance to the cause.

Although I speak of reason, I am fully aware that reason alone will not suffice. Old prisoners do not willingly leave their cells. We shall see whether the youth whom we need are at our command—the youth, who irresistibly draw on the old, carry them forward on strong arms, and transform rational motives into enthusiasm.

II. The Jewish Question

No one can deny the gravity of the situation of the Jews. Wherever they live in perceptible numbers, they are more or less persecuted. Their equality before the law, granted by statute, has become practically a dead letter. They are debarred from filling even moderately high positions, either in the army, or in any public or private capacity. And attempts are made to thrust them out of business also: "Don't buy from Jews!"

Attacks in Parliaments, in assemblies, in the press, in the pulpit, in the street, on journeys—for example, their exclusion from certain hotels—even in places of recreation, become daily more numerous. The forms of persecutions varying according to the countries and social circles in which they occur. In Russia, imposts are levied on Jewish villages; in Rumania, a few persons are put to death; in Germany, they get a good beating occasionally; in Austria, Anti-Semites exercise terrorism over all public life; in Algeria, there are travelling agitators; in Paris, the Jews are shut out of the so-called best social circles and excluded from clubs. Shades of anti-Jewish feeling are innumerable. But this is not to be an attempt to make out a doleful category of Jewish hardships.

I do not intend to arouse sympathetic emotions on our behalf. That would be foolish, futile, and undignified proceeding. I shall content myself with putting the following questions to the Jews: Is it not true that, in countries where we live in perceptible numbers, the position of Jewish lawyers, doctors, technicians, teachers, and employees of all descriptions becomes daily more intolerable? Is it not true, that the Jewish middle classes are seriously threatened? Is it not true, that the passions of the mob are incited against our wealthy people? Is it not true, that our poor endure greater sufferings than any other proletariat? I think that this external pressure makes itself felt everywhere. In our economically upper classes it causes discomfort, in our middle classes continual and grave anxieties, in our lower classes absolute despair.

Everything tends, in fact, to one and the same conclusion, which is clearly enunciated in that classic Berlin phrase: "*Juden Raus!*" (Out with the Jews!)

I shall now put the Question in the briefest possible form: Are we to "get out" now and where to?

Or, may we yet remain? And, how long?

Let us first settle the point of staying where we are. Can we hope for better days, can we possess our souls in patience, can we wait in pious resignation till the princes and peoples of this earth are more mercifully disposed towards us? I say that we cannot hope for a change in the current of feeling. And why not? Even if we were as near to the hearts of princes as are their other subjects, they could not protect us. They would only feel popular hatred by showing us too much favor. By "too much," I really mean less than is claimed as a right by every ordinary citizen, or by every race. The nations in whose midst Jews live are all either covertly or openly Anti-Semitic.

The common people have not, and indeed cannot have, any historic comprehension. They do not know that the sins of the Middle Ages are now being visited on the nations of Europe. We are what the Ghetto made us. We have attained pre-eminence in finance, because mediaeval conditions drove us to it. The same process is now being repeated. We are again being forced into finance, now it is the stock exchange, by being kept out of other branches of economic activity. Being on the stock exchange, we are consequently exposed afresh to contempt. At the same time we continue to produce an abundance of mediocre intellects who find no outlet, and this endangers our social position as much as does our increasing wealth. Educated Jews without means are now rapidly becoming Socialists. Hence we are certain to suffer very severely in the struggle between classes, because we stand in the most exposed position in the camps of both Socialists and capitalists.

PREVIOUS ATTEMPTS AT A SOLUTION

The artificial means heretofore employed to overcome the troubles of Jews have been either too petty—such as attempts at colonization—or attempts to convert the Jews into peasants in their present homes.

What is achieved by transporting a few thousand Jews to another country? Either they come to grief at once, or prosper, and then their prosperity creates Anti-Semitism. We have already discussed these attempts to divert poor Jews to fresh districts. This diversion is clearly inadequate and futile, if it does not actually defeat its own ends; for it merely protracts and postpones a solution, and perhaps even aggravates difficulties.

Whoever would attempt to convert the Jew into a husbandman would be making an extraordinary mistake. For a peasant is in a historical category, as proved by his costume which in some countries he has worn for centuries; and by his tools, which are identical with those used by his earliest forefathers. His plough is unchanged; he carries the seed in his apron; mows with the historical scythe, and threshes with the time-honored flail. But we know that all this can be done by machinery. The agrarian question is only a question of machinery. America must conquer Europe, in the same way as large landed possessions absorb small ones. The peasant is consequently a type which is in course of extinction. Whenever he is artificially preserved, it is done on account of the political interests which he is intended to serve. It is absurd, and indeed impossible, to make modern peasants on the old pattern. No one is wealthy or powerful enough to make civilization take a single retrograde step. The mere preservation of obsolete institutions is a task severe enough to require the enforcement of all the despotic measures of an autocratically governed State.

Are we, therefore, to credit Jews who are intelligent with a desire to become peasants of the old type? One might just as well say to them: "Here is a cross-bow: now go to war!" What? With a cross-bow, while the others have rifles and long range guns? Under these circumstances the Jews are perfectly justified in refusing to stir when people try to make peasants of them. A cross-bow is a beautiful weapon, which inspires me with mournful feelings when I have time to devote to them. But it belongs by rights to a museum.

Now, there certainly are districts to which desperate Jews go out, or at any rate, are willing to go out and till the soil. And a little observation shows that these districts—such as the enclave of Hesse in Germany, and some provinces in Russia—these very districts are the principal seats of Anti-Semitism.

For the world's reformers, who send the Jews to the plough, forget a very important person, who has a great deal to say on the matter. This person is the agriculturist, and the agriculturist is also perfectly justified. For the tax on land, the risks attached to crops, the pressure of large proprietors who cheapen labor, and American competition in particular, combine to make his life hard enough. Besides, the duties on corn cannot go on increasing indefinitely. Nor can the manufacturer be allowed to starve; his political influence is, in fact, in the ascendant, and he must therefore be treated with additional consideration.

All these difficulties are well known, therefore I refer to them only cursorily. I merely wanted to indicate clearly how futile had been past attempts—most of them well intentioned—to solve the Jewish Question.

Neither a diversion of the stream, nor an artificial depression of the intellectual level of our proletariat, will overcome the difficulty. The supposed infallible expedient of assimilation has already been dealt with.

We cannot get the better of Anti-Semitism by any of these methods. It cannot die out so long as its causes are not removed. Are they removable?

CAUSES OF ANTI-SEMITISM

We shall not again touch on those causes which are a result of temperament, prejudice and narrow views, but shall here restrict ourselves to political and economical causes alone. Modern Anti-Semitism is not to be confounded with the religious persecution of the Jews of former times. It does occasionally take a religious bias in some countries, but the main current of the aggressive movement has now changed. In the principal countries where Anti-Semitism prevails, it does so as a result of the emancipation of the Jews. When civilized nations awoke to the inhumanity of discriminatory legislation and enfranchised us, our enfranchisement came too late. It was no longer possible to remove our disabilities in our old homes. For we had, curiously enough, developed while in the Ghetto into a bourgeois people, and we stepped out of it only to enter into fierce competition with the middle classes. Hence, our emancipation set us suddenly within this middle-class circle, where we have a double pressure to sustain, from within and from without. The Christian bourgeoisie would not be unwilling to cast us as a sacrifice to Socialism, though that would not greatly improve matters.

At the same time, the equal rights of Jews before the law cannot be withdrawn where they have once been conceded. Not only because their withdrawal would be opposed to the spirit of our age, but also because it would immediately drive all Jews, rich and poor alike, into the ranks of subversive parties. Nothing effectual can really be done to our injury. In olden days our jewels were seized. How is our movable property to be got hold of now? It consists of printed papers which are locked up somewhere or other in the world, perhaps in the coffers of Christians. It is, of course, possible to get at shares and debentures in railways, banks and industrial undertakings of all descriptions by taxation, and where the progressive income-tax is in force all our movable property can eventually be laid hold of. But all these efforts cannot be directed against Jews alone, and wherever they might nevertheless be made, severe economic crises would be their immediate consequences, which would be by no means confined to the Jews who would be the first affected. The very impossibility of getting at the Jews nourishes and embitters hatred of them. Anti-Semitism increases day by day and hour by hour among the nations; indeed, it is bound to increase, because the causes of its growth continue to exist and cannot be removed. Its remote cause is our loss of the power of assimilation during the Middle Ages; its immediate cause is our excessive production of mediocre intellects, who cannot find an outlet downwards or upwards—that is to say, no wholesome outlet in either direction. When we sink, we become a revolutionary proletariat, the subordinate officers of all revolutionary parties; and at the same time, when we rise, there rises also our terrible power of the purse.

EFFECTS OF ANTI-SEMITISM

The oppression we endure does not improve us, for we are not a whit better than ordinary people. It is true that we do not love our enemies; but he alone who can conquer himself dare reproach us with that fault. Oppression naturally creates hostility against oppressors, and our hostility aggravates the pressure. It is impossible to escape from this eternal circle.

"No!" Some soft-hearted visionaries will say: "No, it is possible! Possible by means of the ultimate perfection of humanity."

Is it necessary to point to the sentimental folly of this view? He who would found his hope for improved conditions on the ultimate perfection of humanity would indeed be relying upon a Utopia!

I referred previously to our "assimilation". I do not for a moment wish to imply that I desire such an end. Our national character is too historically famous, and, in spite of every degradation, too fine to make its annihilation desirable. We might perhaps be able to merge ourselves entirely into surrounding races, if these were to leave us in peace for a period of two generations. But they will not leave us in peace. For a little period they manage to tolerate us, and then their hostility breaks out again and again. The world is provoked somehow by our prosperity, because it has for many centuries been accustomed to consider us as the most contemptible among the poverty-stricken. In its ignorance and narrowness of heart, it fails to observe that prosperity weakens our Judaism and extinguishes our peculiarities. It is only pressure that forces us back to the parent stem; it is only hatred encompassing us that makes us strangers once more.

Thus, whether we like it or not, we are now, and shall henceforth remain, a historic group with unmistakable characteristics common to us all.

We are one people—our enemies have made us one without our consent, as repeatedly happens in history. Distress binds us together, and, thus united, we suddenly discover our strength. Yes, we are strong enough to form a State, and, indeed, a model State. We possess all human and material resources necessary for the purpose.

This is therefore the appropriate place to give an account of what has been somewhat roughly termed our "human material." But it would not be appreciated till the broad lines of the plan, on which everything depends, has first been marked out.

THE PLAN

The whole plan is in its essence perfectly simple, as it must necessarily be if it is to come within the comprehension of all.

Let the sovereignty be granted us over a portion of the globe large enough to satisfy the rightful requirements of a nation; the rest we shall manage for ourselves.

The creation of a new State is neither ridiculous nor impossible. We have in our day witnessed the process in connection with nations which were not largely members of the middle class, but poorer, less educated, and consequently weaker than ourselves. The Governments of all countries scourged by Anti-Semitism will be keenly interested in assisting us to obtain the sovereignty we want.

The plan, simple in design, but complicated in execution, will be carried out by two agencies: The Society of Jews and the Jewish Company.

The Society of Jews will do the preparatory work in the domains of science and politics, which the Jewish Company will afterwards apply practically.

The Jewish Company will be the liquidating agent of the business interests of departing Jews, and will organize commerce and trade in the new country.

We must not imagine the departure of the Jews to be a sudden one. It will be gradual, continuous, and will cover many decades. The poorest will go first to cultivate the soil. In accordance with a preconceived plan, they will construct roads, bridges, railways and telegraph installations; regulate rivers; and build their own dwellings; their labor will create trade, trade will create markets and markets will attract new settlers, for every man will go voluntarily, at his own expense and his own risk. The labor expended on the land will enhance its value, and the Jews will soon perceive that a new and permanent sphere of operation is opening here for that spirit of enterprise which has heretofore met only with hatred and obloquy.

If we wish to found a State today, we shall not do it in the way which would have been the only possible one a thousand years ago. It is foolish to revert to old stages of civilization, as many Zionists would like to do. Supposing, for example, we were obliged to clear a country of wild beasts, we should not set about the task in the fashion of Europeans of the fifth century. We should not take spear and lance and go out singly in pursuit of bears; we would organize a large and active hunting party, drive the animals together, and throw a melinite bomb into their midst.

If we wish to conduct building operations, we shall not plant a mass of stakes and piles on the shore of a lake, but we shall build as men build now. Indeed, we shall build in a bolder and more stately style than was ever adopted before, for we now possess means which men never yet possessed.

The emigrants standing lowest in the economic scale will be slowly followed by those of a higher grade. Those who at this moment are living in despair will go first. They will be led by the mediocre intellects which we produce so superabundantly and which are persecuted everywhere.

This pamphlet will open a general discussion on the Jewish Question, but that does not mean that there will be any voting on it. Such a result would ruin the cause from the outset, and dissidents must remember that allegiance or opposition is entirely voluntary. He who will not come with us should remain behind.

Let all who are willing to join us, fall in behind our banner and fight for our cause with voice and pen and deed.

Those Jews who agree with our idea of a State will attach themselves to the Society, which will thereby be authorized to confer and treat with Governments in the name of our people. The Society will thus be acknowledged in its relations with Governments as a State-creating power. This acknowledgment will practically create the State.

Should the Powers declare themselves willing to admit our sovereignty over a neutral piece of land, then the Society will enter into negotiations for the possession of this land. Here two territories come under consideration, Palestine and Argentine. In both countries important experiments in colonization have been made, though on the mistaken principle of a gradual infiltration of Jews. An infiltration is bound to end badly. It continues till the inevitable moment when the native population feels itself threatened, and forces the Government to stop a further influx of Jews. Immigration is consequently futile unless we have the sovereign right to continue such immigration.

The Society of Jews will treat with the present masters of the land, putting itself under the protectorate of the European Powers, if they prove friendly to the plan. We could offer the present possessors of the land enormous advantages, assume part of the public debt, build new roads for traffic, which our presence in the country would render necessary, and do many other things. The creation of our State would be beneficial to adjacent countries, because the cultivation of a strip of land increases the value of its surrounding districts in innumerable ways.

PALESTINE OR ARGENTINE?

Shall we choose Palestine or Argentine? We shall take what is given us, and what is selected by Jewish public opinion. The Society will determine both these points.

Argentine is one of the most fertile countries in the world, extends over a vast area, has a sparse population and a mild climate. The Argentine Republic would derive considerable profit from the cession of a portion of its territory to us. The present infiltration of Jews has certainly produced some discontent, and it would be necessary to enlighten the Republic on the intrinsic difference of our new movement.

Palestine is our ever-memorable historic home. The very name of Palestine would attract our people with a force of marvellous potency. If His Majesty the Sultan were to give us Palestine, we could in return undertake to regulate the whole finances of Turkey. We should there form a portion of a rampart of Europe against Asia, an outpost of civilization as opposed to barbarism. We should as a neutral State remain in contact with all Europe, which would have to guarantee our existence. The sanctuaries of Christendom would be safeguarded by assigning to them an extraterritorial status such as is well-known to the law of nations. We should form a guard of honor about these sanctuaries, answering for the fulfilment of this duty with our existence. This guard of honor would be the great symbol of the solution of the Jewish Question after eighteen centuries of Jewish suffering.

DEMAND, MEDIUM, TRADE

I said in the last chapter, "The Jewish Company will organize trade and commerce in the new country." I shall here insert a few remarks on that point.

A scheme such as mine is gravely imperilled if it is opposed by "practical" people. Now "practical" people are as a rule nothing more than men sunk into the groove of daily routine, unable to emerge from a narrow circle of antiquated ideas. At the same time, their adverse opinion carries great weight, and can do considerable harm to a new project, at any rate until this new thing is sufficiently strong to throw the "practical" people and their mouldy notions to the winds.

In the earliest period of European railway construction some "practical" people were of the opinion that it was foolish to build certain lines "because there were not even sufficient passengers to fill the mail-coaches." They did not realize the truth—which now seems obvious to us—that travellers do not produce railways, but, conversely, railways produce travellers, the latent demand, of course, is taken for granted.

The impossibility of comprehending how trade and commerce are to be created in a new country which has yet to be acquired and cultivated, may be classed with those doubts of "practical" persons concerning the need of railways. A "practical" person would express himself somewhat in this fashion:

"Granted that the present situation of the Jews is in many places unendurable, and aggravated day by day; granted that there exists a desire to emigrate; granted even that the Jews do emigrate to the new country; how will they earn their living there, and what will they earn? What are they to live on when there? The business of many people cannot be artificially organized in a day."

To this I should reply: We have not the slightest intention of organizing trade artificially, and we should certainly not attempt to do it in a day. But, though the organization of it may be impossible, the promotion of it is not. And how is commerce to be encouraged? Through the medium of a demand. The demand recognized, the medium created, it will establish itself.

If there is a real earnest demand among Jews for an improvement of their status; if the medium to be created—the Jewish Company—is sufficiently powerful, then commerce will extend itself freely in the new country.

III. The Jewish Company

OUTLINES

The Jewish Company is partly modelled on the lines of a great land-acquisition company. It might be called a Jewish Chartered Company, though it cannot exercise sovereign power, and has other than purely colonial tasks.

The Jewish Company will be founded as a joint stock company subject to English jurisdiction, framed according to English laws, and under the protection of England. Its principal center will be London. I cannot tell yet how large the Company's capital should be; I shall leave that calculation to our numerous financiers. But to avoid ambiguity, I shall put it at a thousand million marks (about £50,000,000 or $200,000,000); it may be either more or less than that sum. The form of subscription, which will be further elucidated, will determine what fraction of the whole amount must be paid in at once.

The Jewish Company is an organization with a transitional character. It is strictly a business undertaking, and must be carefully distinguished from the Society of Jews.

The Jewish Company will first of all convert into cash all vested interests left by departing Jews. The method adopted will prevent the occurrences of crises, secure every man's property, and facilitate that inner migration of Christian citizens which has already been indicated.

NON-TRANSFERABLE GOODS

The non-transferable goods which come under consideration are buildings, land, and local business connections. The Jewish Company will at first take upon itself no more than the necessary negotiations for effecting the sale of these goods. These Jewish sales will take place freely and without any serious fall in prices. The Company's branch establishments in various towns will become the central offices for the sale of Jewish estates, and will charge only so much commission on transactions as will ensure their financial stability.

The development of this movement may cause a considerable fall in the prices of landed property, and may eventually make it impossible to find a market for it. At this juncture the Company will enter upon another branch of its functions. It will take over the management of abandoned estates till such time as it can dispose of them to the greatest advantage. It will collect house rents, let out land on lease, and install business managers—these, on account of the required supervision, being, if possible, tenants also. The Company will endeavor everywhere to facilitate the acquisition of land by its tenants, who are Christians. It will, indeed, gradually replace its own officials in the European branches by Christian substitutes (lawyers, etc.); and these are not by any means to become servants of the Jews; they are intended to be free agents to the Christian population, so that everything may be carried through in equity, fairness and justice, and without imperilling the internal welfare of the people.

At the same time the Company will sell estates, or, rather, exchange them. For a house it will offer a house in the new country; and for land, land in the new country; everything being, if possible, transferred to the new soil in the same state as it was in the old. And this transfer will be a great and recognized source of profit to the Company. "Over there" the houses offered in exchange will be newer, more beautiful, and more comfortably fitted, and the landed estates of greater value than those abandoned; but they will cost the Company comparatively little, because it will have bought the ground very cheaply.

PURCHASE OF LAND

The land which the Society of Jews will have secured by international law must, of course, be privately acquired.

Provisions made by individuals for their own settlement do not come within the province of this general account. But the Company will require large areas for its own needs and ours, and these it must secure by centralized purchase. It will negotiate principally for the acquisition of fiscal domains, with the great object of taking possession of this land "over there" without paying a price too high, in the same way as it sells here without accepting one too low. A forcing of prices is not to be considered, because the value of the land will be created by the Company through its organizing the settlement in conjunction with the supervising Society of Jews. The latter will see to it that the enterprise does not become a Panama, but a Suez.

The Company will sell building sites at reasonable rates to its officials, and will allow them to mortgage these for the building of their homes, deducting the amount due from their salaries, or putting it down to their account as increased emolument. This will, in addition to the honors they expect, will be additional pay for their services.

All the immense profits of this speculation in land will go to the Company, which is bound to receive this indefinite premium in return for having borne the risk of the undertaking. When the undertaking involves any risk, the profits must be freely given to those who have borne it. But under no other circumstances will profits be permitted. Financial morality consists in the correlation of risk and profit.

BUILDINGS

The Company will thus barter houses and estates. It must be plain to anyone who has observed the rise in the value of land through its cultivation that the Company will be bound to gain on its landed property. This can best be seen in the case of enclosed pieces of land in town and country. Areas not built over increase in value through surrounding cultivation. The men who carried out the extension of Paris made a successful speculation in land which was ingenious in its simplicity; instead of erecting new buildings in the immediate vicinity of the last houses of the town, they bought up adjacent pieces of land, and began to build on the outskirts of these. This inverse order of construction raised the value of building sites with extraordinary rapidity, and, after having completed the outer ring, they built in the middle of the town on these highly valuable sites, instead of continually erecting houses at the extremity.

Will the Company do its own building, or employ independent architects? It can, and will, do both. It has, as will be shown shortly, an immense reserve of working power, which will not be sweated by the Company, but, transported into brighter and happier conditions of life, will nevertheless not be expensive. Our geologists will have looked to the provision of building materials when they selected the sites of the towns.

What is to be the principle of construction?

WORKMEN'S DWELLINGS

The workmen's dwellings (which include the dwellings of all operatives) will be erected at the Company's own risk and expense. They will resemble neither those melancholy workmen's barracks of European towns, not those miserable rows of shanties which surround factories; they will certainly present a uniform appearance, because the Company must build cheaply where it provides the building materials to a great extent; but the detached houses in little gardens will be united into attractive groups in each locality. The natural conformation of the land will rouse the ingenuity of our young architects, whose ideas have not yet been cramped by routine; and even if the people do not grasp the whole import of the plan, they will at any rate feel at ease in their loose clusters. The Temple will be visible from long distances, for it is only our ancient faith that has kept us together. There will be light, attractive, healthy schools for children, conducted on the most approved modern systems. There will be continuation-schools for workmen, which will educate them in greater technical knowledge and enable them to become intimate with the working of machinery. There will be places of amusement for the proper conduct of which the Society of Jews will be responsible.

We are, however, speaking merely of the buildings at present, and not of what may take place inside of them.

I said that the Company would build workmen's dwellings cheaply. And cheaply, not only because of the proximity of abundant building materials, not only because of the Company's proprietorship of the sites, but also because of the non-payment of workmen.

American farmers work on the system of mutual assistance in the construction of houses. This childishly amicable system, which is as clumsy as the blockhouses erected, can be developed on much finer lines.

UNSKILLED LABORERS

Our unskilled laborers, who will come at first from the great reservoirs of Russia and Rumania, must, of course, render each other assistance, in the construction of houses. They will be obliged to build with wood in the beginning, because iron will not be immediately available. Later on the original, inadequate, makeshift buildings will be replaced by superior dwellings.

Our unskilled laborers will first mutually erect these shelters; and then they will earn their houses as permanent possessions by means of their work—not immediately, but after three years of good conduct. In this way we shall secure energetic and able men, and these men will be practically trained for life by three years of labor under good discipline.

I said before that the Company would not have to pay these unskilled laborers. What will they live on?

On the whole, I am opposed to the Truck system, but it will have to be applied in the case of these first settlers. The Company provides for them in so many ways, that it may take charge of their maintenance. In any case the Truck system will be enforced only during the first few years, and it will benefit the workmen by preventing their being exploited by small traders, landlords, etc. The Company will thus make it impossible from the outset for those of our people, who are perforce hawkers and peddlers here, to reestablish themselves in the same trades over there. And the Company will also keep back drunkards and dissolute men. Then will there be no payment of wages at all during the first period of settlement. Certainly, there will be wages for overtime.

THE SEVEN-HOUR DAY

The seven-hour day is the regular working day.

This does not imply that wood-cutting, digging, stone-breaking, and a hundred other daily tasks should only be performed during seven hours. Indeed not. There will be fourteen hours of labor, work being done in shifts of three and a half hours. The organization of all this will be military in character; there will be commands, promotions and pensions, the means by which these pensions are provided being explained further on.

A sound man can do a great deal of concentrated work in three and a half hours. After an interval of the same length of time—which he will devote to rest, to his family, and to his education under guidance—he will be quite fresh for work again. Such labor can do wonders.

The seven-hour day thus implies fourteen hours of joint labor—more than that cannot be put into a day.

I am convinced that it is quite possible to introduce this seven-hour day with success. The attempts to do so in Belgium and England are well known. Some advanced political economists who have studied the subject, declare that a five-hour day would suffice. The Society of Jews and the Jewish Company will, in any case, make new and extensive experiments which will benefit the other nations of the world; and if the seven-hour day proves itself practicable, it will be introduced in our future State as the legal and regular working day.

Meantime, the Company will always allow its employees the seven-hour day; and it will always be in a position to do so.

The seven-hour day will be the call to summon our people in every part of the world. All must come voluntarily, for ours must indeed be the Promised Land....

Whoever works longer than seven hours receives his additional pay for overtime in cash. Seeing that all his needs are supplied, and that those members of his family who are unable to work are provided for by transplanted and centralized philanthropic institutions, he can save a little money. Thrift, which is already a characteristic of our people, should be greatly encouraged, because it will, in the first place, facilitate the rise of individuals to higher grades; and secondly, the money saved will provide an immense reserve fund for future loans. Overtime will only be permitted on a doctor's certificate, and must not exceed three hours. For our men will crowd to work in the new country, and the world will see then what an industrious people we are.

I shall not describe the mode of carrying out the Truck system, nor, in fact, the innumerable details of any process, for fear of confusing my readers. Women will not be allowed to perform any arduous labor, nor to work overtime.

Pregnant women will be relieved of all work, and will be supplied with nourishing food by the Truck. We want our future generations to be strong men and women.

We shall educate children as we wish from the commencement; but this I shall not elaborate either.

My remarks on workmen's dwellings, and on unskilled laborers and their mode of life, are no more Utopian than the rest of my scheme. Everything I have spoken of is already being put into practice, only on an utterly small scale, neither noticed nor understood. The "Assistance par le Travail," which I learned to know and understand in Paris, was of great service to me in the solution of the Jewish question.

RELIEF BY LABOR

The system of relief by labor which, is now applied in Paris, in many other French towns, in England, in Switzerland, and in America, is a very small thing, but capable of the greatest expansion.

What is the principle of relief by labor?

The principle is: to furnish every needy man with easy, unskilled work, such as chopping wood, or cutting faggots used for lighting stoves in Paris households. This is a kind of prison-work before the crime, done without loss of character. It is meant to prevent men from taking to crime out of want, by providing them with work and testing their willingness to do it. Starvation must never be allowed to drive men to suicide; for such suicides are the deepest disgrace to a civilization which allows rich men to throw tid-bits to their dogs.

Relief by labor thus provides every one with work. But the system has a great defect; there is not a sufficiently large demand for the production of the unskilled workers employed, hence there is a loss to those who employ them; though it is true that the organization is philanthropic, and therefore prepared for loss. But here the benefaction lies only in the difference between the price paid for the work and its actual value. Instead of giving the beggar two sous, the institution supplies him with work on which it loses two sous. But at the same time it converts the good-for-nothing beggar into an honest breadwinner, who has earned perhaps 1 franc 50 centimes. 150 centimes for 10! That is to say, the receiver of a benefaction in which there is nothing humiliating has increased it fifteenfold!

That is to say, fifteen thousand millions for one thousand millions!

The institution certainly loses 10 centimes. But the Jewish Company will not lose one thousand millions; it will draw enormous profits from this expenditure.

There is a moral side also. The small system of relief by labor which exists now preserves rectitude through industry till such time as the man who is out of work finds a post suitable to his capacities, either in his old calling or in a new one. He is allowed a few hours daily for the purpose of looking for a place, in which task the institutions assist him.

The defect of these small organizations, so far, has been that they have been prohibited from entering into competition with timber merchants, etc. Timber merchants are electors; they would protest, and would be justified in protesting. Competition with State prison-labor has also been forbidden, for the State must occupy and feed its criminals.

In fact, there is very little room in an old-established society for the successful application of the system of "Assistance par le Travail."

But there is room in a new society.

For, above all, we require enormous numbers of unskilled laborers to do the first rough work of settlement, to lay down roads, plant trees, level the ground, construct railroads, telegraph installations, etc. All this will be carried out in accordance with a large and previously settled plan.

COMMERCE

The labor carried to the new country will naturally create trade. The first markets will supply only the absolute necessities of life; cattle, grain, working clothes, tools, arms—to mention just a few things. These we shall be obliged at first to procure from neighboring States, or from Europe; but we shall make ourselves independent as soon as possible. The Jewish entrepreneurs will soon realize the business prospects that the new country offers.

The army of the Company's officials will gradually introduce more refined requirements of life. (Officials include officers of our defensive forces, who will always form about a tenth part of our male colonists. They will be sufficiently numerous to quell mutinies, for the majority of our colonists will be peaceably inclined.)

The refined requirements of life introduced by our officials in good positions will create a correspondingly improved market, which will continue to better itself. The married man will send for wife and children, and the single for parents and relatives, as soon as a new home is established "over there." The Jews who emigrate to the United States always proceed in this fashion. As soon as one of them has daily bread and a roof over his head, he sends for his people; for family ties are strong among us. The Society of Jews and the Jewish Company will unite in caring for and strengthening the family still more, not only morally, but materially also. The officials will receive additional pay on marriage and on the birth of children, for we need all who are there, and all who will follow.

OTHER CLASSES OF DWELLINGS

I described before only workmen's dwellings built by themselves, and omitted all mention of other classes of dwellings. These I shall now touch upon. The Company's architects will build for the poorer classes of citizens also, being paid in kind or cash; about a hundred different types of houses will be erected, and, of course, repeated. These beautiful types will form part of our propaganda. The soundness of their construction will be guaranteed by the Company, which will, indeed, gain nothing by selling them to settlers at a fixed sum. And where will these houses be situated? That will be shown in the section dealing with Local Groups.

Seeing that the Company does not wish to earn anything on the building works but only on the land, it will desire as many architects as possible to build by private contract. This system will increase the value of landed property, and it will introduce luxury, which serves many purposes. Luxury encourages arts and industries, paving the way to a future subdivision of large properties.

Rich Jews who are now obliged carefully to secrete their valuables, and to hold their dreary banquets behind lowered curtains, will be able to enjoy their possessions in peace, "over there." If they cooperate in carrying out this emigration scheme, their capital will be rehabilitated and will have served to promote an unexampled undertaking. If in the new settlement rich Jews begin to rebuild their mansions which are stared at in Europe with such envious eyes, it will soon become fashionable to live over there in beautiful modern houses.

SOME FORMS OF LIQUIDATION

The Jewish Company is intended to be the receiver and administrator of the non-transferable goods of the Jews.

Its methods of procedure can be easily imagined in the case of houses and estates, but what methods will it adopt in the transfer of businesses?

Here numberless processes may be found practicable, which cannot all be enlarged on in this outline. But none of them will present any great difficulties, for in each case the business proprietor, when he voluntarily decides to emigrate, will settle with the Company's officers in his district on the most advantageous form of liquidation.

This will most easily be arranged in the case of small employers, in whose trades the personal activity of the proprietor is of chief importance, while goods and organization are a secondary consideration. The Company will provide a certain field of operation for the emigrant's personal activity, and will substitute a piece of ground, with loan of machinery, for his goods.

Jews are known to adapt themselves with remarkable ease to any form of earning a livelihood, and they will quickly learn to carry on a new industry. In this way a number of small traders will become small landholders. The Company will, in fact, be prepared to sustain what appears to be a loss in taking over the non-transferable property of the poorest emigrants; for it will thereby induce the free cultivation of tracts of land, which raises the value of adjacent tracts.

In medium-sized businesses, where goods and organization equal, or even exceed, in importance, the personal activity of the manager, whose larger connection is also non-transferable, various forms of liquidation are possible. Here comes an opportunity for that inner migration of Christian citizens into positions evacuated by Jews. The departing Jew will not lose his personal business credit, but will carry it with him, and make good use of it in a new country to establish himself. The Jewish Company will open a current bank account for him. And he can sell the goodwill of his original business, or hand it over to the control of managers under supervision of the Company's officials. The managers may rent the business or buy it, paying for it by instalments. But the Company acts temporarily as curator for the emigrants, in superintending, through its officers and lawyers, the administration of their affairs, and seeing to the proper collection of all payments.

If a Jew cannot sell his business, or entrust it to a proxy or wish to give up its personal management, he may stay where he is. The Jews who stay will be none the worse off, for they will be relieved of the competition of those who leave, and will no longer hear the Anti-Semitic cry: "Don't buy from Jews!"

If the emigrating business proprietor wishes to carry on his old business in the new country, he can make his arrangements for it from the very commencement. An example will best illustrate my meaning. The firm X carries on a large business in dry goods. The head of the firm wishes to emigrate. He begins by setting up a branch establishment in his future place of residence, and sending out samples of his stock. The first poor settlers will be his first customers; these will be followed by emigrants of a higher class, who require superior goods. X then sends out newer goods, and eventually ships his newest. The branch establishment begins to pay while the principal one is still in existence, so that X ends by having two paying business-houses. He sells his original business or hands it over to his Christian representative to manage, and goes off to take charge of the new one.

Another and greater example: Y and Son are large coal-traders, with mines and factories of their own. How is so huge and complex a property to be liquidated? The mines and everything connected with them might, in the first place, be bought up by the State, in which they are situated. In the second place, the Jewish Company might take them over, paying for them partly in land, partly in cash. A third method might be the conversion of "Y and Son" into a limited company. A fourth method might be the continued working of the business under the original proprietors, who would return at intervals to inspect their property, as foreigners, and as such, under the protection of law in every civilized State. All these suggestions are carried out daily. A fifth and excellent method, and one which might be particularly profitable, I shall merely indicate, because the existing examples of its working are at present few, however ready the modern consciousness may be to adopt them. Y and Son might sell their enterprise to the collective body of their employees, who would form a cooperative society, with limited liability, and might perhaps pay the requisite sum with the help of the State Treasury, which does not charge high interest.

The employees would then gradually pay off the loan, which either the Government or the Jewish Company, or even Y and Son, would have advanced to them.

The Jewish Company will be prepared to conduct the transfer of the smallest affairs equally with the largest. And whilst the Jews quietly emigrate and establish their new homes, the Company acts as the great controlling body, which organizes the departure, takes charge of deserted possessions, guarantees the proper conduct of the movement with its own visible and tangible property, and provides permanent security for those who have already settled.

SECURITIES OF THE COMPANY

What assurance will the Company offer that the abandonment of countries will not cause their impoverishment and produce economic crises?

I have already mentioned that honest Anti-Semites, whilst preserving their independence, will combine with our officials in controlling the transfer of our estates.

But the State revenues might suffer by the loss of a body of taxpayers, who, though little appreciated as citizens, are highly valued in finance. The State should, therefore, receive compensation for this loss. This we offer indirectly by leaving in the country businesses which we have built up by means of Jewish acumen and Jewish industry, by letting our Christian fellow-citizens move into our evacuated positions, and by this facilitating the rise of numbers of people to greater prosperity so peaceably and in so unparalleled a manner. The French Revolution had a somewhat similar result, on a small scale, but it was brought about by bloodshed on the guillotine in every province of France, and on the battlefields of Europe. Moreover, inherited and acquired rights were destroyed, and only cunning buyers enriched themselves by the purchase of State properties.

The Jewish Company will offer to the States that come within its sphere of activity direct as well as indirect advantages. It will give Governments the first offer of abandoned Jewish property, and allow buyers most favorable conditions. Governments, again, will be able to make use of this friendly appropriation of land for the purpose of certain social improvements.

The Jewish Company will give every assistance to Governments and Parliaments in their efforts to direct the inner migration of Christian citizens.

The Jewish Company will also pay heavy taxes. Its central office will be in London, so as to be under the legal protection of a power which is not at present Anti-Semitic. But the Company, if it is supported officially and semi-officially, will everywhere provide a broad basis of taxation. To this end, it will establish taxable branch offices everywhere. Further, it will pay double duties on the two-fold transfer of goods which it accomplishes. Even in transactions where the Company is really nothing more than a real estate agency, it will temporarily appear as a purchaser, and will be set down as the momentary possessor in the register of landed property.

These are, of course, purely calculable matters. It will have to be considered and decided in each place how far the Company can go without running any risks of failure. And the Company itself will confer freely with Finance Ministers on the various points at issue. Ministers will recognize the friendly spirit of our enterprise, and will consequently offer every facility in their power necessary for the successful achievement of the great undertaking.

Further and direct profit will accrue to Governments from the transport of passengers and goods, and where railways are State property the returns will be immediately recognizable. Where they are held by private companies, the Jewish Company will receive favorable terms for transport, in the same way as does every transmitter of goods on a large scale. Freight and carriage must be made as cheap as possible for our people, because every traveller will pay his own expenses. The middle classes will travel with Cook's tickets, the poorer classes in emigrant trains. The Company might make a good deal by reductions on passengers and goods; but here, as elsewhere, it must adhere to its principle of not trying to raise its receipts to a greater sum than will cover its working expenses.

In many places Jews have control of the transport; and the transport businesses will be the first needed by the Company and the first to be liquidated by it. The original owners of these concerns will either enter the Company's service, or establish themselves independently "over there." The new arrivals will certainly require their assistance, and theirs being a paying profession, which they may and indeed must exercise there to earn a living, numbers of these enterprising spirits will depart. It is unnecessary to describe all the business details of this monster expedition. They must be judiciously evolved out of the original plan by many able men, who must apply their minds to achieving the best system.

SOME OF THE COMPANY'S ACTIVITIES

Many activities will be interconnected. For example: the Company will gradually introduce the manufacture of goods into the settlements which will, of course, be extremely primitive at their inception. Clothing, linens, and shoes will first of all be manufactured for our own poor emigrants, who will be provided with new suits of clothing at the various European emigration centers. They will not receive these clothes as alms, which might hurt their pride, but in exchange for old garments: any loss the Company sustains by this transaction will be booked as a business loss. Those who are absolutely without means will pay off their debt to the Company by working overtime at a fair rate of wage.

Existing emigration societies will be able to give valuable assistance here, for they will do for the Company's colonists what they did before for departing Jews. The forms of such cooperation will easily be found.

Even the new clothing of the poor settlers will have the symbolic meaning. "You are now entering on a new life." The Society of Jews will see to it that long before the departure and also during the journey a serious yet festive spirit is fostered by means of prayers, popular lectures, instruction on the object of the expedition, instruction on hygienic matters for their new places of residence, and guidance in regard to their future work. For the Promised Land is the land of work. On their arrival, the emigrants will be welcomed by our chief officials with due solemnity, but without foolish exultation, for the Promised Land will not yet have been conquered. But these poor people should already see that they are at home.

The clothing industries of the Company will, of course, not produce their goods without proper organization. The Society of Jews will obtain from the local branches information about the number, requirements and date of arrival of the settlers, and will communicate all such information in good time to the Jewish Company. In this way it will be possible to provide for them with every precaution.

PROMOTION OF INDUSTRIES

The duties of the Jewish Company and the Society of Jews cannot be kept strictly apart in this outline. These two great bodies will have to work constantly in unison, the Company depending on the moral authority and support of the Society, just as the Society cannot dispense with the material assistance of the Company. For example, in the organizing of the clothing industry, the quantity produced will at first be kept down so as to preserve an equilibrium between supply and demand; and wherever the Company undertakes the organization of new industries the same precaution must be exercised.

But individual enterprise must never be checked by the Company with its superior force. We shall only work collectively when the immense difficulties of the task demand common action; we shall, wherever possible, scrupulously respect the rights of the individual. Private property, which is the economic basis of independence, shall be developed freely and be respected by us. Our first unskilled laborers will at once have the opportunity to work their way up to private proprietorship.

The spirit of enterprise must, indeed, be encouraged in every possible way. Organization of industries will be promoted by a judicious system of duties, by the employment of cheap raw material, and by the institution of a board to collect and publish industrial statistics.

But this spirit of enterprise must be wisely encouraged, and risky speculation must be avoided. Every new industry must be advertised for a long period before establishment, so as to prevent failure on the part of those who might wish to start a similar business six months later. Whenever a new industrial establishment is founded, the Company should be informed, so that all those interested may obtain information from it.

Industrialists will be able to make use of centralized labor agencies, which will only receive a commission large enough to ensure their continuance. The industrialists might, for example, telegraph for 500 unskilled laborers for three days, three weeks, or three months. The labor agency would then collect these 500 unskilled laborers from every possible source, and despatch them at once to carry out the agricultural or industrial enterprise. Parties of workmen will thus be systematically drafted from place to place like a body of troops. These men will, of course, not be sweated, but will work only a seven-hour day; and, in spite of their change of locality, they will preserve their organization, work out their term of service, and receive commands, promotions, and pensions. Some establishments may, of course, be able to obtain their workmen from other sources, if they wish, but they will not find it easy to do so. The Society will be able to prevent the introduction of non-Jewish work-slaves by boycotting obstinate employers, by obstructing traffic, and by various other methods. The seven-hour workers will therefore have to be taken, and we shall thus bring our people gradually, and without coercion, to adopt the normal seven-hour day.

SETTLEMENT OF SKILLED LABORERS

It is clear that what can be done for unskilled workers can be even more easily done for skilled laborers. These will work under similar regulations in the factories, and the central labor agency will provide them when required.

Independent operatives and small employers, must be carefully taught on account of the rapid progress of scientific improvements, must acquire technical knowledge even if no longer very young men, must study the power of water, and appreciate the forces of electricity. Independent workers must also be discovered and supplied by the Society's agency. The local branch will apply, for example, to the central office: "We want so many carpenters, locksmiths, glaziers, etc." The central office will publish this demand, and the proper men will apply there for the work. These would then travel with their families to the place where they were wanted, and would remain there without feeling the pressure of undue competition. A permanent and comfortable home would thus be provided for them.

METHOD OF RAISING CAPITAL

The capital required for establishing the Company was previously put at what seemed an absurdly high figure. The amount actually necessary will be fixed by financiers, and will in any case be a very considerable sum. There are three ways of raising this sum, all of which the Society will take under consideration. This Society, the great "Gestor" of the Jews, will be formed by our best and most upright men, who must not derive any material advantage from their membership. Although the Society cannot at the outset possess any but moral authority, this authority will suffice to establish the credit of the Jewish Company in the nation's eyes. The Jewish Company will be unable to succeed in its enterprise unless it has received the Society's sanction; it will thus not be formed of any mere indiscriminate group of financiers. For the Society will weigh, select and decide, and will not give its approbation till it is sure of the existence of a sound basis for the conscientious carrying out of the scheme. It will not permit experiments with insufficient means, for this undertaking must succeed at the first attempt. Any initial failure would compromise the whole idea for many decades to come, or might even make its realization permanently impossible.

The three methods of raising capital are: (1) Through big banks; (2) Through small and private banks; (3) Through public subscription.

The first method of raising capital is: Through big banks. The required sum could then be raised in the shortest possible time among the large financial groups, after they had discussed the advisability of the course. The great advantage of this method would be that it would avoid the necessity of paying in the thousand millions (to keep to the original figure), immediately in its entirety. A further advantage would be that the credit of these powerful financiers would also be of service to the enterprise. Many latent political forces lie in our financial power, that power which our enemies assert to be so effective. It might be so, but actually it is not. Poor Jews feel only the hatred which this financial power provokes; its use in alleviating their lot as a body, they have not yet felt. The credit of our great Jewish financiers would have to be placed at the service of the National Idea. But should these gentlemen, who are quite satisfied with their lot, feel indisposed to do anything for their fellow-Jews who are unjustly held responsible for the large possessions of certain individuals, then the realization of this plan will afford an opportunity for drawing a clear line of distinction between them and the rest of Jewry.

The great financiers, moreover, will certainly not be asked to raise an amount so enormous out of pure philanthropic motives; that would be expecting too much. The promoters and stock holders of the Jewish Company are, on the contrary, expected to do a good piece of business, and they will be able to calculate beforehand what their chances of success are likely to be. For the Society of Jews will be in possession of all documents and references which may serve to define the prospects of the Jewish Company. The Society will in particular have investigated with exactitude the extent of the new Jewish movement, so as to provide the Company promoters with thoroughly reliable information on the amount of support they may expect. The Society will also supply the Jewish Company with comprehensive modern Jewish statistics, thus doing the work of what is called in France a "societé d'études," which undertakes all preliminary research previous to the financing of a great undertaking. Even so, the enterprise may not receive the valuable assistance of our moneyed magnates. These might, perhaps, even try to oppose the Jewish movement by means of their secret agents. Such opposition we shall meet with relentless determination.

Supposing that these magnates are content simply to turn this scheme down with a smile:

Is it, therefore, done for?

No.

For then the money will be raised in another way—by an appeal to moderately rich Jews. The smaller Jewish banks would have to be united in the name of the National Idea against the big banks till they were gathered into a second and formidable financial force. But, unfortunately, this would require a great deal of financing at first—for the £50,000,000 would have to be subscribed in full before starting work; and, as this sum could only be raised very slowly, all sorts of banking business would have to be done and loans made during the first few years. It might even occur that, in the course of all these transactions, their original object would be forgotten; the moderately rich Jews would have created a new and large business, and Jewish emigration would be forgotten.

The notion of raising money in this way is not by any means impracticable. The experiment of collecting Christian money to form an opposing force to the big banks has already been tried; that one could also oppose them with Jewish money has not been thought of until now.

But these financial conflicts would bring about all sorts of crises; the countries in which they occurred would suffer, and Anti-Semitism would become rampant.

This method is therefore not to be recommended. I have merely suggested it, because it comes up in the course of the logical development of the idea.

I also do not know whether smaller private banks would be willing to adopt it.

In any case, even the refusal of moderately rich Jews would not put an end to the scheme. On the contrary, it would then have to be taken up in real earnest.

The Society of Jews, whose members are not business men, might try to found the Company on a national subscription.

The Company's capital might be raised, without the intermediary of a syndicate, by means of direct subscription on the part of the public. Not only poor Jews, but also Christians who wanted to get rid of them, would subscribe a small amount to this fund. A new and peculiar form of the plebiscite would thus be established, whereby each man who voted for this solution of the Jewish Question would express his opinion by subscribing a stipulated amount. This stipulation would produce security. The funds subscribed would only be paid in if their sum total reached the required amount, otherwise the initial payments would be returned.

But if the whole of the required sum is raised by popular subscription, then each little amount would be secured by the great numbers of other small amounts.

All this would, of course, need the express and definite assistance of interested Governments.

IV. Local Groups

OUR TRANSMIGRATION

Previous chapters explained only how the emigration scheme might be carried out without creating any economic disturbance. But so great a movement cannot take place without inevitably rousing many deep and powerful feelings. There are old customs, old memories that attach us to our homes. We have cradles, we have graves, and we alone know how Jewish hearts cling to the graves. Our cradles we shall carry with us—they hold our future, rosy and smiling. Our beloved graves we must abandon—and I think this abandonment will cost us more than any other sacrifice. But it must be so.

Economic distress, political pressure, and social obloquy have already driven us from our homes and from our graves. We Jews are even now constantly shifting from place to place, a strong current actually carrying us westward over the sea to the United States, where our presence is also not desired. And where will our presence be desired, so long as we are a homeless nation?

But we shall give a home to our people. And we shall give it, not by dragging them ruthlessly out of their sustaining soil, but rather by transplanting them carefully to a better ground. Just as we wish to create new political and economic relations, so we shall preserve as sacred all of the past that is dear to our people's hearts.

Hence a few suggestions must suffice, as this part of my scheme will most probably be condemned as visionary. Yet even this is possible and real, though it now appears to be something vague and aimless. Organization will make of it something rational.

EMIGRATION IN GROUPS

Our people should emigrate in groups of families and friends. But no man will be forced to join the particular group belonging to his former place of residence. Each will be able to journey in his chosen fashion as soon as he has settled his affairs. Seeing that each man will pay his own expenses by rail and boat, he will naturally travel by whatever class suits him best. Possibly there will even be no subdivision for classes on board train and boat, so as to avoid making the poor feel their position too keenly during their long journey. Though we are not exactly organizing a pleasure trip, it is as well to keep them in good humor on the way.

None will travel in penury; on the other hand, all who desire to travel in luxurious ease will be able to follow their bent. Even under favorable circumstances, the movement may not touch certain classes of Jews for several years to come; the intervening period can therefore be employed in selecting the best modes of organizing the journeys. Those who are well off can travel in parties if they wish, taking their personal friends and connections with them. Jews, with the exception of the richest, have, after all, very little intercourse with Christians. In some countries their acquaintance with them is confined to a few spongers, borrowers, and dependents; of a better class of Christian they know nothing. The Ghetto continues though its walls are broken down.

The middle classes will therefore make elaborate and careful preparations for departure. A group of travellers will be formed in each locality, large towns being divided into districts with a group in each district, who will communicate by means of representatives elected for the purpose. This division into districts need not be strictly adhered to; it is merely intended to alleviate the discomfort and homesickness of the poor during their journey outwards. Everybody is free to travel either alone or attached to any local group he prefers. The conditions of travel—regulated according to classes—will apply to all alike. Any sufficiently numerous travelling party can charter a special train and special boat from the Company.

The Company's housing agency will provide quarters for the poorest on their arrival. Later on, when more prosperous emigrants follow, their obvious need for lodgings on first landing will have to be supplied by hotels built by private enterprise. Some of these more prosperous colonists will, indeed, have built their houses before becoming permanent settlers, so that they will merely move from an old home into a new one.

It would be an affront to our intelligent elements to point out everything that they have to do. Every man who attaches himself to the National Idea will know how to spread it, and how to make it real within his sphere of influence. We shall first of all ask for the cooperation of our Rabbis.

OUR RABBIS

Every group will have its Rabbi, travelling with his congregation. Local groups will afterwards form voluntarily about their Rabbi, and each locality will have its spiritual leader. Our Rabbis, on whom we especially call, will devote their energies to the service of our idea, and will inspire their congregations by preaching it from the pulpit. They will not need to address special meetings for the purpose; an appeal such as this may be uttered in the synagogue. And thus it must be done. For we feel our historic affinity only through the faith of our fathers as we have long ago absorbed the languages of different nations to an ineradicable degree.

The Rabbis will receive communications regularly from both Society and Company, and will announce and explain these to their congregations. Israel will pray for us and for itself.

REPRESENTATIVES OF THE LOCAL GROUPS

The local groups will appoint small committees of representative men under the Rabbi's presidency, for discussion and settlement of local affairs.

Philanthropic institutions will be transferred by their local groups, each institution remaining "over there" the property of the same set of people for whom it was originally founded. I think the old buildings should not be sold, but rather devoted to the assistance of indigent Christians in the forsaken towns. The local groups will receive compensation by obtaining free building sites and every facility for reconstruction in the new country.

This transfer of philanthropic institutions will give another of those opportunities, which occur at different points of my scheme, for making an experiment in the service of humanity. Our present unsystematic private philanthropy does little good in proportion to the great expenditure it involves. But these institutions can and must form part of a system by which they will eventually supplement one another. In a new society these organizations can be evolved out of our modern consciousness, and may be based on all previous social experiments. This matter is of great importance to us, on account of our large number of paupers. The weaker characters among us, discouraged by external pressure, spoilt by the soft-hearted charity of our rich men, easily sink until they take to begging.

The Society, supported by the local groups, will give greatest attention to popular education with regard to this particular. It will create a fruitful soil for many powers which now wither uselessly away. Whoever shows a genuine desire to work will be suitably employed. Beggars will not be endured. Whoever refuses to do anything as a free man will be sent to the workhouse.

On the other hand, we shall not relegate the old to an almshouse. An almshouse is one of the cruelest charities which our stupid good nature ever invented. There our old people die out of pure shame and mortification. There they are already buried. But we will leave even to those who stand on the lowest grade of intelligence the consoling illusion of their utility in the world. We will provide easy tasks for those who are incapable of physical labor; for we must allow for diminished vitality in the poor of an already enfeebled generation. But future generations shall be dealt with otherwise; they shall be brought up in liberty for a life of liberty.

We will seek to bestow the moral salvation of work on men of every age and of every class; and thus our people will find their strength again in the land of the seven-hour day.

PLANS OF THE TOWNS

The local groups will delegate their authorized representatives to select sites for towns. In the distribution of land every precaution will be taken to effect a careful transfer with due consideration for acquired rights.

The local groups will have plans of the towns, so that our people may know beforehand where they are to go, in which towns and in which houses they are to live. Comprehensive drafts of the building plans previously referred to will be distributed among the local groups.

The principle of our administration will be strict centralization of our local groups' autonomy. In this way the transfer will be accomplished with the minimum of pain.

I do not imagine all this to be easier than it actually is; on the other hand, people must not imagine it to be more difficult than it is in reality.

THE DEPARTURE OF THE MIDDLE CLASSES

The middle classes will involuntarily be drawn into the outgoing current, for their sons will be officials of the Society or employees of the Company "over there." Lawyers, doctors, technicians of every description, young business people—in fact, all Jews who are in search of opportunities, who now escape from oppression in their native country to earn a living in foreign lands—will assemble on a soil so full of fair promise. The daughters of the middle classes will marry these ambitious men. One of them will send for his wife or fiancee to come out to him, another for his parents, brothers and sisters. Members of a new civilization marry young. This will promote general morality and ensure sturdiness in the new generation; and thus we shall have no delicate offspring of late marriages, children of fathers who spent their strength in the struggle for life.

Every middle-class emigrant will draw more of his kind after him.

The bravest will naturally get the best out of the new world.

But there we seem undoubtedly to have touched on the crucial difficulty of my plan.

Even if we succeeded in opening a world discussion on the Jewish Question in a serious manner—

Even if this debate led us to a positive conclusion that the Jewish State were necessary to the world—

Even if the Powers assisted us in acquiring the sovereignty over a strip of territory—

How are we to transport masses of Jews without undue compulsion from their present homes to this new country?

Their emigration is surely intended to be voluntary.

THE PHENOMENON OF MULTITUDES

Great exertions will hardly be necessary to spur on the movement. Anti-Semites provide the requisite impetus. They need only do what they did before, and then they will create a desire to emigrate where it did not previously exist, and strengthen it where it existed before. Jews who now remain in Anti-Semitic countries do so chiefly because even those among them who are most ignorant of history know that numerous changes of residence in bygone centuries never brought them any permanent good. Any land which welcomed the Jews today, and offered them even fewer advantages than that which the Jewish State would guarantee them, would immediately attract a great influx of our people. The poorest, who have nothing to lose would drag themselves there. But I maintain, and every man may ask himself whether I am not right, that the pressure weighing on us arouses a desire to emigrate even among prosperous strata of society. Now our poorest strata alone would suffice to found a State;

these form the strongest human material for acquiring a land, because a little despair is indispensable to the formation of a great undertaking.

But when our "desperados" increase the value of the land by their presence and by the labor they expend on it, they make it at the same time increasingly attractive as a place of settlement to people who are better off.

Higher and yet higher strata will feel tempted to go over. The expedition of the first and poorest settlers will be conducted by Company and Society conjointly, and will probably be additionally supported by existing emigration and Zionist societies.

How may a number of people be directed to a particular spot without being given express orders to go there? There are certain Jewish benefactors on a large scale who try to alleviate the sufferings of the Jews by Zionist experiments. To them this problem also presented itself, and they thought to solve it by giving the emigrants money or means of employment. Thus the philanthropists said: "We pay these people to go there."

Such a procedure is utterly wrong, and all the money in the world will not achieve its purpose.

On the other hand, the Company will say: "We shall not pay them, we shall let them pay us. We shall merely offer them some inducements to go."

A fanciful illustration will make my meaning more explicit: One of those philanthropists (whom we will call "The Baron") and myself both wish to get a crowd of people on to the plain of Longchamps near Paris, on a hot Sunday afternoon. The Baron, by promising them

10 francs each, will, for 200,000 francs, bring out 20,000 perspiring and miserable people, who will curse him for having given them so much annoyance. Whereas I will offer these 200,000 francs as a prize for the swiftest racehorse—and then I shall have to put up barriers to keep the people off Longchamps. They will pay to go in: 1 franc, 5 francs, 20 francs.

The consequence will be that I shall get the half-a-million of people out there; the President of the Republic will drive up "a la Daumont"; and the crowds will enjoy and amuse themselves. Most of them will think it an agreeable walk in the open air in spite of heat and dust; and I shall have made by my 200,000 francs about a million in entrance money and taxes on gaming. I shall get the same people out there whenever I like but the Baron will not—not on any account.

I will give a more serious illustration of the phenomenon of multitudes where they are earning a livelihood. Let any man attempt to cry through the streets of a town: "Whoever is willing to stand all day long through a winter's terrible cold, through a summer's tormenting heat, in an iron hall exposed on all sides, there to address every passer-by, and to offer him fancy wares, or fish, or fruit, will receive two florins, or four francs or something similar."

How many people would go to the hall? How many days would they hold out when hunger drove them there? And if they held out, what energy would they display in trying to persuade passers-by to buy fish, fruit and fancy wares?

We shall set about it in a different way. In places where trade is active, and these places we shall the more easily discover, since we ourselves direct trade withersoever we wish, in these places we shall build large halls, and call them markets. These halls might be worse built and more unwholesome than those above mentioned, and yet people would stream towards them. But we shall use our best efforts, and we shall build them better, and make them more beautiful than the first. And the people, to whom we had promised nothing, because we cannot promise anything without deceiving them, these excellent, keen business men will gaily create most active commercial intercourse. They will harangue the buyers unweariedly; they will stand on their feet, and scarcely think of fatigue. They will hurry off at dawn, so as to be first on the spot; they will form unions, cartels, anything to continue bread-winning undisturbed. And if they find at the end of the day that all their hard work has produced only 1 florin, 50 kreutzer, or 3 francs, or something similar, they will yet look forward hopefully to the next day, which may, perhaps, bring them better luck.

We have given them hope.

Would any one ask whence the demand comes which creates the market? Is it really necessary to tell them again?

I pointed out that by means of the system "Assistance par le Travail" the return could be increased fifteenfold. One million would produce fifteen millions; and one thousand millions, fifteen thousand millions.

This may be the case on a small scale; is it so on a large one? Capital surely yields a return diminishing in inverse ratio to its own growth. Inactive and inert capital yields this diminishing return, but active capital brings in a marvellously increasing return. Herein lies the social question.

Am I stating a fact? I call on the richest Jews as witnesses of my veracity. Why do they carry on so many different industries? Why do they send men to work underground and to raise coal amid terrible dangers for meagre pay? I cannot imagine this to be pleasant, even for the owners of the mines. For I do not believe that capitalists are heartless, and I do not pretend that I believe it. My desire is not to accentuate, but to smooth differences.

Is it necessary to illustrate the phenomenon of multitudes, and their concentration on a particular spot by references to pious pilgrimages?

I do not want to hurt anyone's religious sensibility by words which might be wrongly interpreted.

I shall merely refer quite briefly to the Mohammedan pilgrimages to Mecca, the Catholic pilgrimages to Lourdes, and to many other spots whence men return comforted by their faith, and to the holy Hock at Trier. Thus we shall also create a center for the deep religious needs of our people. Our ministers will understand us first, and will be with us in this.

We shall let every man find salvation "over there" in his own particular way. Above and before all we shall make room for the immortal band of our Freethinkers, who are continually making new conquests for humanity.

No more force will be exercised on any one than is necessary for the preservation of the State and order;

and the requisite force will not be arbitrarily defined by one or more shifting authorities; it will be fixed by iron laws.

Now, if the illustrations I gave make people draw the inference that a multitude can be only temporarily attracted to centers of faith, of business, or of amusement, the reply to their objection is simple. Whereas one of these objects by itself would certainly only attract the masses, all these centers of attraction combined would be calculated permanently to hold and satisfy them. For all these centers together form a single, great, long-sought object, which our people has always longed to attain, for which it has kept itself alive, for which it has been kept alive by external pressure—a free home! When the movement commences, we shall draw some men after us and let others follow; others again will be swept into the current, and the last will be thrust after us.

These last hesitating settlers will be the worst off, both here and there.

But the first, who go over with faith, enthusiasm, and courage will have the best positions.

OUR HUMAN MATERIAL

There are more mistaken notions abroad concerning Jews than concerning any other people. And we have become so depressed and discouraged by our historic sufferings that we ourselves repeat and believe these mistakes. One of these is that we have an immoderate love of business. Now it is well known that wherever we are permitted to take part in the rising of classes, we give up our business as soon as possible. The great majority of Jewish business men give their sons a superior education. Hence, the so-called "Judaizing" of all intellectual professions. But even in economically feebler grades of society, our love of trade is not so predominant as is generally supposed. In the Eastern countries of Europe there are great numbers of Jews who are not traders, and who are not afraid of hard work either. The Society of Jews will be in a position to prepare scientifically accurate statistics of our human forces. The new tasks and prospects that await our people in the new country will satisfy our present handicraftsmen, and will transform many present small traders into manual workers.

A peddler who travels about the country with a heavy pack on his back is not so contented as his persecutors imagine. The seven-hour day will convert all of his kind into workmen. They are good, misunderstood people, who now suffer perhaps more severely than any others. The Society of Jews will, moreover, busy itself from the outset with their training as artisans. Their love of gain will be encouraged in a healthy manner. Jews are of a thrifty and adaptable disposition, and are qualified for any means of earning a living, and it will therefore suffice to make small trading unremunerative, to cause even present peddlers to give it up altogether. This could be brought about, for example, by encouraging large department stores which provide all necessaries of life. These general stores are already crushing small trading in large cities. In a land of new civilization they will absolutely prevent its existence. The establishment of these stores is further advantageous, because it makes the country immediately habitable for people who require more refined necessaries of life.

HABITS

Is a reference to the little habits and comforts of the ordinary man in keeping with the serious nature of this pamphlet?

I think it is in keeping, and, moreover, very important. For these little habits are the thousand and one fine delicate threads which together go to make up an unbreakable rope.

Here certain limited notions must be set aside. Whoever has seen anything of the world knows that just these little daily customs can easily be transplanted everywhere. The technical contrivances of our day, which this scheme intends to employ in the service of humanity, have heretofore been principally used for our little habits. There are English hotels in Egypt and on the mountain-crest in Switzerland, Vienna cafes in South Africa, French theatres in Russia, German operas in America, and best Bavarian beer in Paris.

When we journey out of Egypt again we shall not leave the fleshpots behind.

Every man will find his customs again in the local groups, but they will be better, more beautiful, and more agreeable than before.

V. Society of Jews and Jewish State

NEGOTIORUM GESTIO

This pamphlet is not intended for lawyers. I can therefore touch only cursorily, as on so many other things, upon my theory of the legal basis of a State.

I must, nevertheless, lay some stress on my new theory, which could be maintained, I believe, even in discussion with men well versed in jurisprudence.

According to Rousseau's now antiquated view, a State is formed by a social contract. Rousseau held that: "The conditions of this contract are so precisely defined by the nature of the agreement that the slightest alteration would make them null and void. The consequence is that, even where they are not expressly stated, they are everywhere identical, and everywhere tacitly accepted and recognized," etc.

A logical and historic refutation of Rousseau's theory was never, nor is now, difficult, however terrible and far-reaching its effects may have been. The question whether a social contract with "conditions not expressly stated, yet unalterable," existed before the framing of a constitution, is of no practical interest to States under modern forms of government. The legal relationship between government and citizen is in any case clearly established now.

But previous to the framing of a constitution, and during the creation of a new State, these principles assume great practical importance. We know and see for ourselves that States still continue to be created. Colonies secede from the mother country. Vassals fall away from their suzerain; newly opened territories are immediately formed into free States. It is true that the Jewish State is conceived as a peculiarly modern structure on unspecified territory. But a State is formed, not by pieces of land, but rather by a number of men united under sovereign rule.

The people is the subjective, land the objective foundation of a State, and the subjective basis is the more important of the two. One sovereignty, for example, which has no objective basis at all, is perhaps the most respected one in the world. I refer to the sovereignty of the Pope.

The theory of rationality is the one at present accepted in political science. This theory suffices to justify the creation of a State, and cannot be historically refuted in the same way as the theory of a contract. Insofar as I am concerned only with the creation of a Jewish State, I am well within the limits of the theory of rationality. But when I touch upon the legal basis of the State, I have exceeded them. The theories of a divine institution, or of superior power, or of a contract, and the patriarchal and patrimonial theories do not accord with modern views. The legal basis of a State is sought either too much within men (patriarchal theory, and theories of superior force and contract), or too far above them (divine institution), or too far below them (objective patrimonial theory). The theory of rationality leaves this question conveniently and carefully unanswered. But a question which has seriously occupied doctors of jurisprudence in every age cannot be an absolutely idle one. As a matter of fact, a mixture of human and superhuman goes to the making of a State. Some legal basis is indispensable to explain the somewhat oppressive relationship in which subjects occasionally stand to rulers. I believe it is to be found in the *negotiorum gestio*, wherein the body of citizens represents the *dominus negotiorum*, and the government represents the *gestor*.

The Romans, with their marvellous sense of justice, produced that noble masterpiece, the *negotiorum gestio*. When the property of an oppressed person is in danger, any man may step forward to save it. This man is the *gestor*, the director of affairs not strictly his own. He has received no warrant—that is, no human warrant; higher obligations authorize him to act. The higher obligations may be formulated in different ways for the State, and so as to respond to individual degrees of culture attained by a growing general power of comprehension. The *gestio* is intended to work for the good of the *dominus*—the people, to whom the *gestor* himself belongs.

The *gestor* administers property of which he is joint-owner. His joint proprietorship teaches him what urgency would warrant his intervention, and would demand his leadership in peace or war; but under no circumstances is his authority valid *qua* joint proprietorship. The consent of the numerous joint-owners is even under most favorable conditions a matter of conjecture.

A State is created by a nation's struggle for existence. In any such struggle it is impossible to obtain proper authority in circumstantial fashion beforehand. In fact, any previous attempt to obtain a regular decision from the majority would probably ruin the undertaking from the outset. For internal schisms would make the people defenceless against external dangers. We cannot all be of one mind; the *gestor* will therefore simply take the leadership into his hands and march in the van.

The action of the *gestor* of the State is sufficiently warranted if the common cause is in danger, and the *dominus* is prevented, either by want of will or by some other reason, from helping itself.

But the *gestor* becomes similar to the *dominus* by his intervention, and is bound by the agreement *quasi ex contractu*. This is the legal relationship existing before, or, more correctly, created simultaneously with the State.

The *gestor* thus becomes answerable for every form of negligence, even for the failure of business undertakings, and the neglect of such affairs as are intimately connected with them, etc. I shall not further enlarge on the *negotiorum gestio*, but rather leave it to the State, else it would take us too far from the main subject. One remark only: "Business management, if it is approved by the owner, is just as effectual as if it had originally been carried on by his authority."

And how does all this affect our case?

The Jewish people are at present prevented by the Diaspora from conducting their political affairs themselves. Besides, they are in a condition of more or less severe distress in many parts of the world. They need, above all things a *gestor*. This *gestor* cannot, of course, be a single individual. Such a one would either make himself ridiculous, or—seeing that he would appear to be working for his own interests—contemptible.

The *gestor* of the Jews must therefore be a body corporate.

And that is the Society of Jews.

THE GESTOR OF THE JEWS

This organ of the national movement, the nature and functions of which we are at last dealing with, will, in fact, be created before everything else. Its formation is perfectly simple. It will take shape among those energetic Jews to whom I imparted my scheme in London.

The Society will have scientific and political tasks, for the founding of a Jewish State, as I conceive it, presupposes the application of scientific methods. We cannot journey out of Egypt today in the primitive fashion of ancient times. We shall previously obtain an accurate account of our number and strength. The undertaking of that great and ancient *gestor* of the Jews in primitive days bears much the same relation to ours that some wonderful melody bears to a modern opera. We are playing the same melody with many more violins, flutes, harps, violoncellos, and bass viols; with electric light, decorations, choirs, beautiful costumes, and with the first singers of their day.

This pamphlet is intended to open a general discussion on the Jewish Question. Friends and foes will take part in it; but it will no longer, I hope, take the form of violent abuse or of sentimental vindication, but of a debate, practical, large, earnest, and political.

The Society of Jews will gather all available declarations of statesmen, parliaments, Jewish communities, societies, whether expressed in speeches or writings, in meetings, newspapers or books.

Thus the Society will find out for the first time whether the Jews really wish to go to the Promised Land, and whether they must go there. Every Jewish community in the world will send contributions to the Society towards a comprehensive collection of Jewish statistics.

Further tasks, such as investigation by experts of the new country and its natural resources, the uniform planning of migration and settlement, preliminary work for legislation and administration, etc., must be rationally evolved out of the original scheme.

Externally, the Society will attempt, as I explained before in the general part, to be acknowledged as a

State-forming power. The free assent of many Jews will confer on it the requisite authority in its relations with Governments.

Internally, that is to say, in its relation with the Jewish people, the Society will create all the first indispensable institutions; it will be the nucleus out of which the public institutions of the Jewish State will later on be developed.

Our first object is, as I said before, supremacy, assured to us by international law, over a portion of the globe sufficiently large to satisfy our just requirements.

What is the next step?

THE OCCUPATION OF THE LAND

When nations wandered in historic times, they let chance carry them, draw them, fling them hither and thither, and like swarms of locusts they settled down indifferently anywhere. For in historic times the earth was not known to man. But this modern Jewish migration must proceed in accordance with scientific principles.

Not more than forty years ago gold-digging was carried on in an extraordinarily primitive fashion. What adventurous days were those in California! A report brought desperados together from every quarter of the earth; they stole pieces of land, robbed each other of gold, and finally gambled it away, as robbers do.

But today! What is gold-digging like in the Transvaal today? Adventurous vagabonds are not there; sedate geologists and engineers alone are on the spot to regulate its gold industry, and to employ ingenious machinery in separating the ore from surrounding rock. Little is left to chance now.

Thus we must investigate and take possession of the new Jewish country by means of every modern expedient.

As soon as we have secured the land, we shall send over a ship, having on board the representatives of the Society, of the Company, and of the local groups, who will enter into possession at once.

These men will have three tasks to perform: (1) An accurate, scientific investigation of all natural resources of the country; (2) the organization of a strictly centralized administration; (3) the distribution of land. These tasks intersect one another, and will all be carried out in conformity with the now familiar object in view.

One thing remains to be explained—namely, how the occupation of land according to local groups is to take place.

In America the occupation of newly opened territory is set about in naive fashion. The settlers assemble on the frontier, and at the appointed time make a simultaneous and violent rush for their portions.

We shall not proceed thus to the new land of the Jews. The lots in provinces and towns will be sold by auction, and paid for, not in money, but in work. The general plan will have settled on streets, bridges, waterworks, etc., necessary for traffic. These will be united into provinces. Within these provinces sites for towns will be similarly sold by auction. The local groups will pledge themselves to carry the business property through, and will cover the cost by means of self-imposed assessments. The Society will be in a position to judge whether the local groups are not venturing on sacrifices too great for their means. The large communities will receive large sites for their activity. Great sacrifices will thus be rewarded by the establishment of universities, technical schools, academies, research institutes, etc., and these Government institutes, which do not have to be concentrated in the capital, will be distributed over the country.

The personal interest of the buyers, and, if necessary, the local assessment, will guarantee the proper working of what has been taken over. In the same way, as we cannot, and indeed do not wish to obliterate distinctions between single individuals, so the differences between local groups will also continue. Everything will shape itself quite naturally. All acquired rights will be protected, and every new development will be given sufficient scope.

Our people will be made thoroughly acquainted with all these matters.

We shall not take others unawares or mislead them, any more than we shall deceive ourselves.

Everything must be systematically settled beforehand. I merely indicate this scheme: our keenest thinkers will combine in elaborating it. Every social and technical achievement of our age and of the more advanced age which will be reached before the slow execution of my plan is accomplished must be employed for this object. Every valuable invention which exists now, or lies in the future, must be used. By these means a country can be occupied and a State founded in a manner as yet unknown to history, and with possibilities of success such, as never occurred before.

CONSTITUTION

One of the great commissions which the Society will have to appoint will be the council of State jurists. These must formulate the best, that is, the best modern constitution possible. I believe that a good constitution should be of moderately elastic nature. In another work I have explained in detail what forms of government I hold to be the best. I think a democratic monarchy and an aristocratic republic are the finest forms of a State, because in them the form of State and the principle of government are opposed to each other, and thus preserve a true balance of power. I am a staunch supporter of monarchial institutions, because these allow of a continuous policy, and represent the interests of a historically famous family born and educated to rule, whose desires are bound up with the preservation of the State. But our history has been too long interrupted for us to attempt direct continuity of ancient constitutional forms, without exposing ourselves to the charge of absurdity.

A democracy without a sovereign's useful counterpoise is extreme in appreciation and condemnation, tends to idle discussion in Parliaments, and produces that objectionable class of men—professional politicians. Nations are also really not fit for unlimited democracy at present, and will become less and less fitted for it in the future. For a pure democracy presupposes a predominance of simple customs, and our customs become daily more complex with the growth of commerce and increase of culture. *"Le ressort d'une democratic est la vertu,"* said wise Montesquieu. And where is this virtue, that is to say, this political virtue, to be met with? I do not believe in our political virtue; first, because we are no better than the rest of modern humanity; and, secondly, because freedom will make us show our fighting qualities at first. I also hold a settling of questions by the referendum to be an unsatisfactory procedure, because there are no simple political questions which can be answered merely by Yes and No. The masses are also more prone even than Parliaments to be led away by heterodox opinions, and to be swayed by vigorous ranting. It is impossible to formulate a wise internal or external policy in a popular assembly.

Politics must take shape in the upper strata and work downwards. But no member of the Jewish State will be oppressed, every man will be able and will wish to rise in it. Thus a great upward tendency will pass through our people; every individual by trying to raise himself, raising also the whole body of citizens. The ascent will take a normal form, useful to the State and serviceable to the National Idea.

Hence I incline to an aristocratic republic. This would satisfy the ambitious spirit in our people, which has now degenerated into petty vanity. Many of the institutions of Venice pass through my mind; but all that which caused the ruin of Venice must be carefully avoided. We shall learn from the historic mistakes of others, in the same way as we learn from our own; for we are a modern nation, and wish to be the most modern in the world. Our people, who are receiving the new country from the Society, will also thankfully accept the new constitution it offers them. Should any opposition manifest itself, the Society will suppress it. The Society cannot permit the exercise of its functions to be interpreted by short-sighted or ill-disposed individuals.

LANGUAGE

It might be suggested that our want of a common current language would present difficulties. We cannot converse with one another in Hebrew. Who amongst us has a sufficient acquaintance with Hebrew to ask for a railway ticket in that language? Such a thing cannot be done. Yet the difficulty is very easily circumvented. Every man can preserve the language in which his thoughts are at home. Switzerland affords a conclusive proof of the possibility of a federation of tongues. We shall remain in the new country what we now are here, and we shall never cease to cherish with sadness the memory of the native land out of which we have been driven.

We shall give up using those miserable stunted jargons, those Ghetto languages which we still employ, for these were the stealthy tongues of prisoners. Our national teachers will give due attention to this matter; and the language which proves itself to be of greatest utility for general intercourse will be adopted without compulsion as our national tongue. Our community of race is peculiar and unique, for we are bound together only by the faith of our fathers.

THEOCRACY

Shall we end by having a theocracy? No, indeed. Faith unites us, knowledge gives us freedom. We shall therefore prevent any theocratic tendencies from coming to the fore on the part of our priesthood. We shall keep our priests within the confines of their temples in the same way as we shall keep our professional army within the confines of their barracks. Army and priesthood shall receive honors high as their valuable functions deserve. But they must not interfere in the administration of the State which confers distinction upon them, else they will conjure up difficulties without and within.

Every man will be as free and undisturbed in his faith or his disbelief as he is in his nationality. And if it should occur that men of other creeds and different nationalities come to live amongst us, we should accord them honorable protection and equality before the law. We have learnt toleration in Europe. This is not sarcastically said; for the Anti-Semitism of today could only in a very few places be taken for old religious intolerance. It is for the most part a movement among civilized nations by which they try to chase away the spectres of their own past.

LAWS

When the idea of a State begins to approach realization, the Society of Jews will appoint a council of jurists to do the preparatory work of legislation. During the transition period these must act on the principle that every emigrant Jew is to be judged according to the laws of the country which he has left. But they must try to bring about a unification of these various laws to form a modern system of legislation based on the best portions of previous systems. This might become a typical codification, embodying all the just social claims of the present day.

THE ARMY

The Jewish State is conceived as a neutral one. It will therefore require only a professional army, equipped, of course, with every requisite of modern warfare, to preserve order internally and externally.

THE FLAG

We have no flag, and we need one. If we desire to lead many men, we must raise a symbol above their heads.

I would suggest a white flag, with seven golden stars. The white field symbolizes our pure new life; the stars are the seven golden hours of our working-day. For we shall march into the Promised Land carrying the badge of honor.

RECIPROCITY AND EXTRADITION TREATIES

The new Jewish State must be properly founded, with due regard to our future honorable position in the world. Therefore every obligation in the old country must be scrupulously fulfilled before leaving. The Society of Jews and the Jewish Company will grant cheap passage and certain advantages in settlement to those only who can present an official testimonial from the local authorities, certifying that they have left their affairs in good order.

Every just private claim originating in the abandoned countries will be heard more readily in the Jewish State than anywhere else. We shall not wait for reciprocity; we shall act purely for the sake of our own honor. We shall thus perhaps find, later on, that law courts will be more willing to hear our claims than now seems to be the case in some places.

It will be inferred, as a matter of course, from previous remarks, that we shall deliver up Jewish criminals more readily than any other State would do, till the time comes when we can enforce our penal code on the same principles as every other civilized nation does. There will therefore be a period of transition, during which we shall receive our criminals only after they have suffered due penalties. But, having made amends, they will be received without any restrictions whatever, for our criminals also must enter upon a new life.

Thus emigration may become to many Jews a crisis with a happy issue. Bad external circumstances, which ruin many a character, will be removed, and this change may mean salvation to many who are lost.

Here I should like briefly to relate a story I came across in an account of the gold mines of Witwatersrand. One day a man came to the Rand, settled there, tried his hand at various things, with the exception of gold mining, till he founded an ice factory, which did well. He soon won universal esteem by his respectability, but after some years he was suddenly arrested. He had committed some defalcations as banker in Frankfort, had fled from there, and had begun a new life under an assumed name. But when he was led away as prisoner, the most respected people in the place appeared at the station, bade him a cordial farewell and *au revoir*—for he was certain to return.

How much this story reveals! A new life can regenerate even criminals, and we have a proportionately small number of these. Some interesting statistics on this point are worth reading, entitled "The Criminality of Jews in Germany," by Dr. P. Nathan, of Berlin, who was commissioned by the "Society for Defense against Anti-Semitism" to make a collection of statistics based on official returns. It is true that this pamphlet, which teems with figures, has been prompted, as many another "defence," by the error that Anti-Semitism can be refuted by reasonable arguments. We are probably disliked as much for our gifts as we are for our faults.

BENEFITS OF THE EMIGRATION OF THE JEWS

I imagine that Governments will, either voluntarily or under pressure from the Anti-Semites, pay certain attention to this scheme, and they may perhaps actually receive it here and there with a sympathy which they will also show to the Society of Jews.

For the emigration which I suggest will not create any economic crises. Such crises as would follow everywhere in consequence of Jew-baiting would rather be prevented by the carrying out of my plan. A great period of prosperity would commence in countries which are now Anti-Semitic. For there will be, as I have repeatedly said, an internal migration of Christian citizens into the positions slowly and systematically evacuated by the Jews. If we are not merely suffered, but actually assisted to do this, the movement will have a generally beneficial effect. That is a narrow view, from which one should free oneself, which sees in the departure of many Jews a consequent impoverishment of countries. It is different from a departure which is a result of persecution, for then property is indeed destroyed, as it is ruined in the confusion of war. Different again is the peaceable voluntary departure of colonists, wherein everything is carried out with due consideration for acquired rights, and with absolute conformity to law, openly and by light of day, under the eyes of the authorities and the control of public opinion. The emigration of Christian proletarians to different parts of the world would be brought to a standstill by the Jewish movement.

The States would have a further advantage in the enormous increase of their export trade; for, since the emigrant Jews "over there" would depend for a long time to come on European productions, they would necessarily have to import them. The local groups would keep up a just balance, and the customary needs would have to be supplied for a long time at the accustomed places.

Another, and perhaps one of the greatest advantages, would be the ensuing social relief. Social dissatisfaction would be appeased during the twenty or more years which the emigration of the Jews would occupy, and would in any case be set at rest during the whole transition period.

The shape which the social question may take depends entirely on the development of our technical resources. Steampower concentrated men in factories about machinery where they were overcrowded, and where they made one another miserable by overcrowding. Our present enormous, injudicious, and unsystematic rate of production is the cause of continual severe crises which ruin both employers and employees. Steam crowded men together; electricity will probably scatter them again, and may perhaps bring about a more prosperous condition of the labor market. In any case our technical inventors, who are the true benefactors of humanity, will continue their labors after the commencement of the emigration of the Jews, and they will discover things as marvellous as those we have already seen, or indeed more wonderful even than these.

The word "impossible" has ceased to exist in the vocabulary of technical science. Were a man who lived in the last century to return to the earth, he would find the life of today full of incomprehensible magic. Wherever the moderns appear with our inventions, we transform the desert into a garden. To build a city takes in our time as many years as it formerly required centuries; America offers endless examples of this. Distance has ceased to be an obstacle. The spirit of our age has gathered fabulous treasures into its storehouse. Every day this wealth increases. A hundred thousand heads are occupied with speculations and research at every point of the globe, and what any one discovers belongs the next moment to the whole world. We ourselves will use and carry on every new attempt in our Jewish land; and just as we shall introduce the seven-hour day as an experiment for the good of humanity, so we shall proceed in everything else in the same humane spirit, making of the new land a land of experiments and a model State.

After the departure of the Jews the undertakings which they have created will remain where they originally were found. And the Jewish spirit of enterprise will not even fail where people welcome it. For Jewish capitalists will be glad to invest their funds where they are familiar with surrounding conditions.

And whereas Jewish money is now sent out of countries on account of existing persecutions, and is sunk in most distant foreign undertakings, it will flow back again in consequence of this peaceable solution, and will contribute to the further progress of the countries which the Jews have left.

VI. Conclusion

How much has been left unexplained, how many defects, how many harmful superficialities, and how many useless repetitions in this pamphlet, which I have thought over so long and so often revised!

But a fair-minded reader, who has sufficient understanding to grasp the spirit of my words, will not be repelled by these defects. He will rather be roused thereby to cooperate with his intelligence and energy in a work which is not one man's task alone, and to improve it.

Have I not explained obvious things and overlooked important objections?

I have tried to meet certain objections; but I know that many more will be made, based on high grounds and low.

To the first class of objections belongs the remark that the Jews are not the only people in the world who are in a condition of distress. Here I would reply that we may as well begin by removing a little of this misery, even if it should at first be no more than our own.

It might further be said that we ought not to create new distinctions between people; we ought not to raise fresh barriers, we should rather make the old disappear. But men who think in this way are amiable visionaries; and the idea of a native land will still flourish when the dust of their bones will have vanished tracelessly in the winds. Universal brotherhood is not even a beautiful dream. Antagonism is essential to man's greatest efforts.

But the Jews, once settled in their own State, would probably have no more enemies. As for those who remain behind, since prosperity enfeebles and causes them to diminish, they would soon disappear altogether. I think the Jews will always have sufficient enemies, such as every nation has. But once fixed in their own land, it will no longer be possible for them to scatter all over the world. The diaspora cannot be reborn, unless the civilization of the whole earth should collapse; and such a consummation could be feared by none but foolish men. Our present civilization possesses weapons powerful enough for its self-defense.

Innumerable objections will be based on low grounds, for there are more low men than noble in this world. I have tried to remove some of these narrow-minded notions; and whoever is willing to fall in behind our white flag with its seven stars, must assist in this campaign of enlightenment. Perhaps we shall have to fight first of all against many an evil-disposed, narrow-hearted, short-sighted member of our own race.

Again, people will say that I am furnishing the Anti-Semites with weapons. Why so? Because I admit the truth? Because I do not maintain that there are none but excellent men against us?

Will not people say that I am showing our enemies the way to injure us? This I absolutely dispute. My proposal could only be carried out with the free consent of a majority of Jews. Action may be taken against individuals or even against groups of the most powerful Jews, but Governments will never take action against all Jews. The equal rights of the Jew before the law cannot be withdrawn where they have once been conceded; for the first attempt at withdrawal would immediately drive all Jews, rich and poor alike, into the ranks of revolutionary parties. The beginning of any official acts of injustice against the Jews invariably brings about economic crises. Therefore, no weapons can be effectually used against us, because these injure the hands that wield them. Meantime hatred grows apace. The rich do not feel it much, but our poor do. Let us ask our poor, who have been more severely proletarized since the last removal of Anti-Semitism than ever before.

Some of our prosperous men may say that the pressure is not yet severe enough to justify emigration, and that every forcible expulsion shows how unwilling our people are to depart. True, because they do not know where to go; because they only pass from one trouble into another. But we are showing them the way to the Promised Land; and the splendid force of enthusiasm must fight against the terrible force of habit.

Persecutions are no longer so malignant as they were in the Middle Ages? True, but our sensitiveness has increased, so that we feel no diminution in our sufferings; prolonged persecution has overstrained our nerves.

Will people say, again, that our enterprise is hopeless, because even if we obtained the land with supremacy over it, the poor only would go with us? It is precisely the poorest whom we need at first. Only the desperate make good conquerors.

Will some one say: Were it feasible it would have been done long ago?

It has never yet been possible; now it is possible. A hundred—or even fifty years ago it would have been nothing more than a dream. Today it may become a reality. Our rich, who have a pleasurable acquaintance with all our technical achievements, know full well how much money can do. And thus it will be; just the poor and simple, who do not know what power man already exercises over the forces of Nature, just these will have the firmest faith in the new message. For these have never lost their hope of the Promised Land.

Here it is, fellow Jews! Neither fable nor deception! Every man may test its reality for himself, for every man will carry over with him a portion of the Promised

Land—one in his head, another in his arms, another in his acquired possessions.

Now, all this may appear to be an interminably long affair. Even in the most favorable circumstances, many years might elapse before the commencement of the foundation of the State. In the meantime, Jews in a thousand different places would suffer insults, mortifications, abuse, blows, depredation, and death. No; if we only begin to carry out the plans, Anti-Semitism would stop at once and for ever. For it is the conclusion of peace.

The news of the formation of our Jewish Company will be carried in a single day to the remotest ends of the earth by the lightning speed of our telegraph wires.

And immediate relief will ensue. The intellects which we produce so superabundantly in our middle classes will find an outlet in our first organizations, as our first technicians, officers, professors, officials, lawyers, and doctors; and thus the movement will continue in swift but smooth progression.

Prayers will be offered up for the success of our work in temples and in churches also; for it will bring relief from an old burden, which all have suffered.

But we must first bring enlightenment to men's minds. The idea must make its way into the most distant, miserable holes where our people dwell. They will awaken from gloomy brooding, for into their lives will come a new significance. Every man need think only of himself, and the movement will assume vast proportions.

And what glory awaits those who fight unselfishly for the cause!

Therefore I believe that a wondrous generation of Jews will spring into existence. The Maccabeans will rise again.

Let me repeat once more my opening words: The Jews who wish for a State will have it.

We shall live at last as free men on our own soil, and die peacefully in our own homes.

The world will be freed by our liberty, enriched by our wealth, magnified by our greatness.

And whatever we attempt there to accomplish for our own welfare, will react powerfully and beneficially for the good of humanity.

Printed in Dunstable, United Kingdom